W9-BNX-993

Strange Scriptures
that
Perplex the Western Mind

CLARIFIED IN THE LIGHT OF CUSTOMS AND CONDITIONS
IN BIBLE LANDS

by

BARBARA M. BOWEN

Bob Jones University, Greenville, S. C.

WM. B. EERDMANS PUBLISHING COMPANY
Grand Rapids   Michigan

102652

STRANGE SCRIPTURES THAT PERPLEX
THE WESTERN MIND
By Barbara M. Bowen

Copyright, 1944, *by*
Barbara M. Bowen

All rights in this book are reserved. No part may be reproduced
in any manner without permission in writing from the publisher,
except brief quotations used in connection with a review in a
magazine or newspaper.

Set up and printed, July 1940

Reprinted, August 1985

ISBN 0-8028-1511-1

PRINTED IN THE UNITED STATES OF AMERICA

DEDICATED

to the companion of all my journeys,
my partner in work and study,
my husband,

Frank Henry Bowen

CONTENTS

CONTENTS — Continued

CONTENTS — Continued

CONTENTS — Continued

CONTENTS—Continued

FOREWORD

Frequently after our lectures on the land and the people of the country of our Lord, people have requested us to bring together in a book some of the customs and thoughts and ways of these people that appear strange to us.

Palestine has changed very little since Bible days, the people are chiefly Ishmaelites and dress, eat, live and think as their ancestors did. They live this very primitive life because their parents and grandparents for a hundred generations have lived so.

They say, "Our father Abraham lived as we do, what was good for him is good for us; what was good enough for yesterday is good enough for tomorrow."

A better understanding of their lives, their homes, their dress, their work and their ways of thinking will help us to comprehend many Scriptures that now appear strange.

This small book contains nothing new, but brings together information on many customs differing so widely from those of our part of the world that we hope it will help Sunday School teachers and young people to a little better understanding of some parts of THE BOOK.

— BARBARA M. BOWEN

*Strange Scriptures That Perplex
the Modern Mind*

Table or **Scamba.** A stool on which the native places his food and by which he sits to eat.

"They uncovered the roof." (Mark 2:4). A native village home.

"With a writer's inkhorn by his side." A native woman having a letter written for her by a Scribe.

"He washed their feet." (John 13:6). An **Ibrick** and **Tuskt** for the washing of feet on entering the house and washing the hands after meals.

Tear Bottles. "She bathed His feet with tears."

CHAPTER 1

PERPLEXING SCRIPTURES

"Salute No Man by the Way"
(Luke 10:4)

JESUS is sending out the seventy, two by two, into every city and place where He himself would come. He tells them that the harvest is very great but there are few laborers. He tells them to carry neither purse, nor scrip, nor shoes; and to *salute no man by the way.*

This sounds to our ears rather impolite and not like Jesus, who was kind and friendly. We are accustomed only to the manners of the Western world and we think merely of a nod of the head, a smile, or a grasp of the hand, which takes very little time.

Why did Christ command the seventy to salute no man by the way? They were on very important business, going out as messengers for their King and they must not loiter in idle conversation with the people they would meet on the way.

If a peasant from the Bible Lands should come to our country and watch us hurrying to catch a train and see us nod to a friend as a salutation, he certainly would consider us extremely impolite. No peasant would ever be so rude. When he walks through a town or village and meets an acquaintance, he rushes up to him and falls on his neck and kisses him on both cheeks, as the father of the prodigal son

17

did. Then they each lay the right hand over the heart, then on their lips, and then slowly raise it to the forehead; and after that clasp each other's hands.

Placing the hand over the heart is saying, "With my heart I love you"; placing the hand on the lips is saying, "With my lips I give you the kiss of friendship"; while raising the hand to the forehead signifies, "I esteem and respect you." Next they exchange greetings and inquire after each other's welfare. Then they question each other with complimentary speeches which would take, at the very least, another half hour, and they embrace again and depart.

Time is of no importance to these villagers and you never saw one hurry. They frequently stand by the hour repeating over and over the same words, such as, "Is there peace with thee? Is there peace with thy house?"

When we read in the Bible, "Is it well?" the meaning is, "Is there peace?" Gen. 37:14: "And he said to him, Go I pray thee, see whether it be well with thy brethren, and well with the flocks." This is also found in many other places in the Bible.

Because of this very common custom of such long greetings, Elisha said to his servant Gehazi, "If thou meet any man, salute him not" (II Kings 4:29).

Salutations today are just as lovely as in Old Testament days. When you meet a friend in any of the Bible Lands, he exclaims, "Peace be unto you." When he leaves you he will say, "God go with you" — "Mar salaam," to a man; "Mar salaami," to a woman. You reply, "Peace remain with you" — "Allah selmack," to a man; "Allah selmick," to a woman.

A native may be just longing to kill you, and yet when you meet him on the street, he will stop and greet you thus: "May your days be blessed! God give you health and smooth your path! Peace to your lives. Go in peace." The Bible has many salutations which are common today in

Bible Lands. When the angel Gabriel appeared to Mary in Nazareth to announce to her that she was to be the mother of the Messiah, Mary was troubled in her mind to know what manner of salutation the angel used — was it the usual form, was it flattery, or had it a real meaning?

There is scarcely a salutation found in the Bible that may not be heard spoken every day in the villages of Palestine. All this helps us better to understand why Christ said to the disciples, "Salute no man by the way."

"Go Not From House to House"
(Luke 10:4-7)

"And whatsoever house ye enter into, there abide."

Christ sends out the seventy helpers with these instructions: "Carry neither purse nor scrip nor shoes: and salute no man by the way. And into whatsoever house ye enter ... in the same house remain, eating and drinking such things as they give: for the labourer is worthy of his hire."

This sounds strange to our ears, but remember there were many people to carry the Good News to, and not much time left in which to accomplish this work.

When a stranger arrived in a village or an encampment, the people, one after another, must invite him to eat with them. There is a very strict custom about it, involving much hypocrisy; and any failure to observe this law of hospitality is violently resented by all the neighborhood, and often leads to feuds. This hospitality consumes an enormous amount of time, leads to levity and gossip, and in every way would counteract the success of the spiritual mission on which the disciples were sent.

On account of all these obstacles, the helpers were instructed to avoid all these feasts. Christ was sending them out, not to be honored and feasted, but to call men to repentance. They were, therefore, first to find a suitable place to lodge in, and to remain there until their work for the Lord in that village was accomplished. "Go not from house to house, carry no scrip." The scrip is the whole skin of a kid, dried. It is fastened to the belt or a cord, and is thrown over the shoulder under the outer garment. The traveler will carry in this scrip bread, figs and olives, enough to last on his journey. The disciples were told not to take scrip or food with them (Luke 9:3).

"Suffer Me First to Bury My Father"
(Matt. 8:21; Luke 9:59)

"And Jesus said to a man, Follow me. But he said, Lord, suffer me first to go and bury my father. And the Lord replied, Let the dead bury their dead." This answer appears to us very harsh and unsympathetic. We see in our mind a young man grieving for a dead father and wishing naturally to remain near him, and Jesus calls him, and the young man refuses the call.

The Palestinian understands this as being nothing in the world but an excuse, and an exceedingly common one in that country. No doubt the father was perfectly well and strong, but the son did not want to follow Christ, and as was the common custom, he answered, "No, I cannot, my father is dead and I must bury him."

If you ask some natives even today to do anything they do not want to do, they will not answer that they do not feel well, or haven't the time, but they will instantly say to you, "No, I cannot, my father is dead."

"The Lord Hath Made Bare His Arm"
(Isaiah 52:10)

"The Lord hath made bare His holy arm in the eyes of all the nations; and all the ends of the earth shall see the salvation of our God."

The meaning of this Scripture is clear, but the vividness of it is hidden unless one has seen the women of the Bible Lands taking their long flowing sleeves, tying the ends in a knot, and throwing them over their shoulders to leave the arms bare so they can work unhindered.

The men will do the same with the long sleeves of their *kamise,* tie the ends together and throw them over their heads, so that they can go out to fight and not be hindered by long pointed sleeves.

"The Lord hath made bare his arm."

"He Shall Dwell Between His Shoulders"
(Deut. 33:12)

"The beloved of the Lord shall dwell in safety by him; and the Lord shall cover him all the day long, and he shall dwell between his shoulders."

This Scripture refers to the Bible Lands' hammock or cradle, made of camel's hair, and used by the village mothers and the mothers of the tent dwellers. It is a hammock about two by two and a half feet, with a strong cord at either end, so that it may be carried on the mother's shoulders, with the cords passing across her forehead.

In the field the mother suspends the little hammock from the limb of a tree, or if there is no tree, she erects a tripod of sticks from which the hammock hangs, covering the baby's face with one of her own garments to protect the child from the sun and flies.

How often we have seen a small hammock on the shoulders of a young mother, with a tiny face peeking out, or more often with a sleeping baby and a little foot or a small hand showing at the side of the hammock.

When the mother carries the child, she will draw a part of her large white veil over the hammock as a protection against the hot sun, either partly or completely covering it.

This is the common picture referred to in Deut. 36:12: "The beloved of the Lord shall dwell safely by him; and the Lord shall cover him all the day long, and he shall dwell between his shoulders."

"Thy Youth Renewed Like the Eagle's"
(Psalm 103:5)

"Who satisfieth thy mouth with good things; so that thy youth is renewed as the eagle's."

This fact in the life of the eagle is given as a promise to the righteous. The eagle lives to a very great age. As he grows old his beak becomes so long that he can no longer eat; then he flies away by himself to the top of a cliff and pecks and pecks on a rock until his bill falls off, after which a new bill grows in its place. While without the use of his bill, the bird also loses his feathers because of fasting. After the new bill grows and he again takes food, new feathers start growing, so that he looks and appears like a young eagle, going forth in a new covering with youthful beauty and strength. "Thy youth is renewed as the eagle's."

"The Eagle Stirreth Up Her Nest"
(Deut. 32:11)

"As the eagle stirreth up her nest, fluttereth over her young, spreadeth abroad her wings, taketh them, beareth them on her wings."

Moses is telling the people how God deals with his children. The mother eagle watches her baby eaglets carefully; as they grow, she stirs them up a bit so they will not be contented to lie in the nest: she then flutters over them to make them want to use their wings as she does; then she pushes them out of the nest and flies down beneath, carefully watching them so no harm will come to her children. When her mother eye sees the little wings growing

weary, she spreads out her great strong wings; catches them
and bears them back to the nest for rest.

The nest is always very high. A fall would mean the end
of flying, but the mother eagle knows when it is time to
shake the young out of the nest and when to fly down to
bring them back.

That is what God does for us, bears us on eagle's wings.

"And David Danced Before the Lord"
(II Sam. 6:14)

"And David danced before the Lord with all his might:
and David was girded with a linen ephod."

At the head of a great procession there would frequently
be seen a half naked buffoon dancing, going through ges-
ticulations usual on such occasions. It was all done in hon-
or of the person to whom the procession was made, and was
the office of a slave only.

King David and all the house of Israel brought up the
ark of the Lord with shouting and with trumpets; and
David danced before the Lord, he took the place of a slave
at the head of the procession to do honor to Jehovah.

Michal, King David's wife, not understanding her husband's motive, and thinking he had lowered himself before
the people, reproached him bitterly, and despised him in
her heart.

"Bathed His Feet With Tears"
(Luke 7:38)

"She began to wash his feet with tears, and did wipe
them with the hairs of her head."

We find reference in many old books to the custom of collecting the tears of the whole family and preserving them
in bottles. Thus King David prays, "Put thou my tears into thy bottle: are they not in thy book?" Tear bottles have

been found in very large numbers on opening ancient tombs. They are made of thin glass usually, although the very poor sometimes had just simple pottery bottles, not even baked or glazed. They were all made with a slender body, broad at the base, with a funnel-shaped top. Every member of the family owned a tear bottle and they collected the tears of the whole family.

When serious trouble or a death occured in the home, all the relatives came and each one brought his tear bottle with him. As they wept and wailed, the tears rolling down their cheeks, each person took his or her tear bottle and gathered tears from the faces of all present.

This bottle was exceedingly sacred to them. It represented all the heartaches, sorrows and bereavements from the grandparents down to the small child. When a person died, his tear bottle was buried with him, as one of his most sacred possessions.

This helps us to a better understanding of what the woman did for her Master. She noticed the very discourteous way in which Christ was treated as a guest in the house of Simon the Pharisee.

He provided no water to wash the Lord's feet and no oil to anoint his head; so this poor, sinful woman, longing for forgiveness and a new life, took her tear bottle, poured the tears over his tired, dusty feet and wiped them with her long hair. A great sacrifice indeed, done in love and gratitude to the Saviour. They could not be replaced and she might die without a bottle of tears to be buried with her in her tomb.

"She bathed his feet with tears."

"Water on the Hands of Elijah"
(II Kings 3:11)

"Here is Elisha, who poured water on the hands of Elijah."

The same practice prevails to this day. Nowhere is water poured into a basin, but the servant pours water from a pitcher on the hands of his master. Washing of feet was very common, and, in a hot country where sandals were worn, would be essential to comfort. "Moab is my washpot" (Psa. 60:8). Moab was doomed to the most abject and degrading servitude.

In the practice of washing the feet there was the combination of humility with affectionate attention; and the Savior washed his disciples' feet, designing by a symbolic action to teach an important truth. If the Master had performed an office so needful and yet so lowly, how much more were the disciples themselves bound to consider any Christian service whatever as a duty, which each was to perform for the other! Love dignifies any service.

Cursing the Fig Tree
(Mark 11:12-14; 20-23)

While Jesus was on earth He was constantly teaching His disciples by parables.

One strange thing about the fig tree is that the fruit appears before the leaves. If the first fruit did not appear, there would be no other figs on the tree.

Christ and the disciples were passing and looked for some of the small but sweet first fruit. It was a tree with leaves, it looked well and useful, but it was a useless tree, and not only that, it led the passerby to believe it was a good tree, when it was of no value.

It was a type of profession without productiveness. Our Lord could not endure hypocrisy in any one or any thing, and condemned it more than any other sin. Here Christ is giving His disciples an illustration they would not easily forget.

A person might say this fig tree did not belong to our Savior, and therefore He had no right to take the fruit. We can answer this by reference to the Mosaic law in such cases. "You are not to prohibit those that pass by, when your fruits are ripe, to touch them, but to give them leave to fill themselves full of what you have." And the custom of plucking ripe figs as you pass by the orchards is still universal in the Bible lands, especially from trees not inclosed. After the feast in September, the figs which remain on the trees are common property and the poor may enter the orchards and take all they want.

Lying at the Feet
(Ruth 3:7-14)

Ruth, when reaping in the field of Boaz, went to the resting place of Boaz, uncovered his feet, and lying crosswise, covered herself with his cloak or skirt, a custom common all over the East. By doing so, Ruth just placed herself under the protection of Boaz; later she asked Boaz to spread his skirt over her. She only asked him to acknowledge her right to his protection.

Boaz replied, "I will do to thee all that thou requirest, for all the city doth know that thou art a virtuous women. If thy kinsman will not take thee to wife, I will." This same custom is referred to in Ezekiel 16:8: "I will spread my skirt over thee, and thou becomest mine."

"Bring the Veil Which Thou Hast Upon Thee"
(Ruth 3:15)

"Boaz said, Bring the veil that thou hast upon thee, and hold it . . . he measured six measures of barley, and laid it on her: and she went into the city."

Whenever a woman of the Bible Lands today lacks a basket or bag, the veil comes into use. She places what she has to carry in one end of her long veil, gathers and ties it around with one corner, and places it on the top of her head. Veils have always been used by the women to carry burdens in.

People unacquainted with the ancient customs of these lands may wonder how Ruth's veil could hold so much grain. We think of a veil as being small and made of gauze or net, but not so in Palestine. The *khirka,* as the veil is called, is made of very strong material, six feet or more in length and all of four feet wide. The woman places it over her cap, covering her entire headgear, except the coins in front. It is considered very immodest for a woman to have her head or hair exposed in public. When at home where she is seen only by her family, the veil is removed.

Usually veils are made of very heavy white linen, embroidered in colors on the ends, while in the district north of Jerusalem each girl makes a veil for herself almost covered with beautiful needlework, so that it will correspond with the white embroidered *tobe,* or dress for her marriage.

"The Wringing of Milk Bringeth Forth Butter"
(Prov. 30:33)

"Surely the churning of milk bringeth forth butter, and the wringing of the nose bringeth forth blood; so the forcing of wrath bringeth forth strife." But the word for "churning" and "wringing" is the same in Hebrew. It is the *wringing* of milk that bringeth forth butter, just as these women are squeezing and wringing this milk in the "bottle." There is no analogy between *our* mode of *churning* and pulling a man's nose until the blood comes, but in the Arab operation the comparison is quite natural and emphatic.

What are these women kneading and shaking in that large black bag, suspended from this three-legged crotch? That is a bottle, not a bag, made by stripping off the entire skin of a young fuffalo. It is full of milk, and that is their way of churning. When the butter "has come," they take it out, boil or melt it, and then put it into *bottles* made of goats' skins. In winter it resembles candied honey, in summer it is mere oil.

Quails

(Num. 11:31, 32)

"And there went forth a wind from the Lord, and brought forth quails from the sea, and let them fall by the camp, as it were a day's journey on this side, and as it were a day's journey on the other side, round about the camp, and as it were two cubits high upon the face of the earth."

The correct rendering is "about two cubits above the face of the earth," that is within reach of the people that might slay them for food. The statement is not that the quails were piled up from the face of the earth two cubits deep. The level of their flight was two cubits *above* the earth. "And it came to pass, that at even the quails came up, and covered the camp: and in the morning the dew lay round about the host."

The quail is a bird of the grouse family. They are abundant in all the temperate regions of Europe and western Asia, migrating to and from Africa at the proper season. In the spring they are found in great numbers in the Syrian deserts and Arabia. An immense supply was furnished the Israelites on two occasions (Exodus 16:13; Numbers 11:31, 32). Both were at the season of migration, and the birds were caught in such quantities as to suffice for a million people for a month. They were dried in the sun, and preserved with salt.

Bosom

(Isa. 40:11)

In the East people usually carry within a fold of their robe things that could not be carried in the hand. Isaiah tells us that the Savior will carry the lambs in His bosom. Lazarus is spoken of as in Abraham's bosom. We get the idea of a banquet. Lazarus, an ulcerated and crippled

THE LOST COIN
A Bethlehem woman's silver dowry.

TWO WOMEN AT THE MILL
The grinding of the mill is the sweetest music
to the Oriental ear.

beggar, who had lain at the rich man's gate, contented with the scraps thrown out to him, was translated to a feast, and he had the most intimate place among all the guests, reclining on the host's bosom. Christ is in the bosom of the Father; that is, He possesses the closest intimacy with the Father.

The Jews reclined at meals. By this arrangement, the head of one person was brought almost into the bosom of the person who lay above him, and the guests were arranged so as to bring the most honored nearest to the host.

The dinner bed was used by the Romans as well as by Jews. It had couches built around it. Each man, in order to feed himself, lay nearly flat on his breast, and stretched out his hands toward the table; but afterwards, when his hunger was satisfied, he turned on his left side, leaning on his elbow. Each person was provided with a cushion or bolster on which to support the upper part of his body on a raised position; as the left arm soon became weary. The lower part of his body was extended diagonally, with the feet outwards. We can see how the woman who was a sinner might come behind Christ and bathe his feet with tears and anoint them. (Luke 7:37, 38)

Anointing

(Psalm 104:15)

"Oil to make the face to shine." The earliest use of anointing of which we know is told us in Genesis 28:18. Also we read in Gen. 31:13: "I am the God of Bethel, where thou anointest the pillar." The pouring of oil on the stone which had been Jacob's pillow was for the purpose of consecration to the service of God. High priests and sacred vessels were anointed for the same reason. The king was called "the Lord's anointed," anointed for the service of God.

The oil was carefully prepared for all such purposes and could not be used for any ordinary occasion. Directions for making this oil are found in Exodus 30:23-33. It was composed of myrrh, sweet cinnamon and sweet calamus and of olive oil.

Anointing was also used on festive occasions. It was the mark of attention paid to guests, here we have the phase "anointed with the oil of gladness." In Egypt it was customary for a servant to anoint the head of every guest and the omission was considered a sign of mourning.

In Luke 7:38, 46, the host neglected to anoint the head of Jesus and provided no water for His feet. Not only was oil used for the head, but also for the skin. In many countries the use of oil for the body is believed to strengthen it and to protect it from the heat of the sun. The bodies of the dead were often anointed to preserve them.

Ashes

(Gen. 18:27)

Ashes, in the symbolic language of Scripture, denotes human frailty, as in Genesis 18:27: "I have taken upon me to speak unto the Lord, who am but dust and ashes;" *deep humiliation,* as in Esther 4:1: "Mordecai rent his clothes, and put on sackcloth with ashes." To sit in ashes was a token of *mourning,* as in Job 2:8: "And he sat down among the ashes." Feeding on ashes appears to express grief. Psalm 102:9: "For I have eaten ashes like bread and mingled my bread with weeping." There was a sort of lustral water, made with the ashes of the heifer sacrificed on the great day of expiation. These ashes were distributed to the people, and the water as well as the ashes used in purification for sin, and running water shall be put thereto in a vessel: And a clean person shall take hyssop, and dip it in the water, and sprinkle it upon the tent, and upon the persons that were there, and upon him that touched a bone, or one slain, or one dead, or a grave."

Whited Sepulchres
(Matt. 23:27)

As in ancient times, so today white-washed tombs mark the place of the dead. They all receive a new whitening before days or seasons of feasting and worship. The people believed that to touch or come in contact with a tomb was to defile oneself. Death was the result of sin, and, therefore caused contamination. Therefore supulchres were always whitewashed. That made them to be easily seen and avoided.

Christ made reference to this practice in an address to the scribes and Pharisees. Whitewashing a tombstone did not change the nature of the grave itself, it still contained dead man's bones. The thing might be made attractive without, but there was no difference within. Christ insisted that religion was not to be an outward decoration merely, just for special occasions; it was to be a life principle, giving reality to all we do.

"Woe unto you, scribes and Pharisees, hypocrites, for ye are like whited sepulchres."

Coals of Fire
(Rom. 12:20)

The Scriptures have much to say about forgiving our enemies. Paul says that if we give food and drink to our enemies, "we shall be heaping coals of fine on their heads." To us this doesn't sound like forgiveness, but like taking vengeance. In the Bible lands almost everything is carried on the head—water jars, baskets of fruit, vegetables, fish or any other article. Those carrying the burden rarely touch it with the hands, and they walk through crowded streets and lanes with perfect ease. In many homes the only fire they have is kept in a brazier which they use for simple cooking as well as for warmth.

They plan to always keep it burning. If it should go out, some member of the family will take the brazier to a neighbor's house to borrow fire. Then she will lift the brazier to her head and start for home. If her neighbor is a generous woman, she will heap the brazier full of coals. To feed an enemy and give him drink was like heaping the empty brazier with live coals,—which meant food, warmth, and almost life itself to the person or home needing it and was the symbol of finest generosity.

"Thou shalt heap coals of fire on his head."

Selah

This word occurs seventy-five times in the Psalms and three times in Habakkuk. It is derived from a Hebrew word which means *to be silent,* and signifies *to pause* in the singing. It is to direct the singer to pause or be silent while the instruments played interlude.

A Covenant of Salt
(Num. 18:19)

"It is a covenant of salt forever before the Lord unto thee and to thy seed with thee."

This act of eating another's salt has always been regarded as a token of fidelity and friendship. Sometimes bread and salt are eaten together, making a covenant. "There is bread and salt between us, we are brothers." The custom came down from the remotest antiquity. The covenant can never be forgotten nor renounced.

CHAPTER 2

WOMEN

"Who Can Find a Virtuous Woman?"
(Prov. 31:10)

LET us look into some native homes and see if Solomon's estimation of the Bible Lands' woman holds good today.

"The heart of her husband doth safely trust in her." The husband in most cases, does not feel very sure that, "she will do him good and not evil," so he sets a jealous watch over her, and places every valuable he owns under lock and key.

Two things are responsible — bad education, and lack of love. The girl is kept in ignorance, and married while still a child without regard to the affections of her heart. How can a husband expect to trust in a wife so ignorant and one obtained in such a manner?

A Contentious Woman
(Prov. 27:15, 16)

A continual dropping on a very rainy day and a contentious woman are alike, said Solomon. Whosoever hideth her hideth the wind, and the ointment of his right hand, which betrayeth itself. The force of this proverb is well understood in all its details in Palestine. Such rains as they have thoroughly soak through the flat roofs of those homes, and the water descends in numberless leaks all over the room. This continual dropping — tuk, tuk, all day and all night, is the most annoying thing in the world, unless it is the ceaseless clatter of a contentious woman.

Let me describe a quarrel I heard part of, and these people would rather quarrel than eat, about anything or mere nothing.

A quarrel started between two neighbor women about a chicken one owned. It lasted fourteen hours. Through all this long period, the "contentious woman" ceased not to scream, scold, curse her enemy in a very original way, and so loud that the whole neighborhood could understand every word. She would run into the room where her victim was, then rush out again, run around the court like a maniac, tear off her veil and tarbouch, tear her hair, pound her chest, screaming as loud as she could all the time. She would stop and get her old shoes and throw them at her victim, all the time trembling like a leaf. Nothing could stop her, until finally she became run down like a clock.

The Ointment of the Right Hand
(Prov. 27:16)

This refers to a very common custom still frequent these days. The odors of their perfumes is so very powerful that the very street where the people walk is scented. Such ointment cannot be hidden. The right hand, being the most honorable, is used in anointing and cannot be hidden in the bosom, as all the salutations and endless gestures are made with the right hand.

These people will tell you that the right hand belongs to God and the left hand to the devil, so they are exceedingly careful to use the right hand. I terribly offended a native by waving my left hand to her, as I would do at home.

"The ointment of the right hand will betray itself; so will a contentious woman, she cannot be hid."

Two Women at the Mill
(Math. 24:41)

Usually two women sit facing each other at the mill, both holding the handle by which the upper is turned round on the "nether" millstone. One of the women whose right hand is disengaged, throws in the grain as needed through the hole in the upper stone. Both women keep their hold on the handle, and pull to, or push from, as two men do with a crosscut saw. Men never grind at the mill. It is very fatiguing work, and only slaves or the lowest servants, or the wives are ever set at grinding.

This grinding at the mill was often imposed upon captives taken in war. In this way Samson was horribly abused by the Philistines, made to grind at the mill like a slave or a woman.

The mill is the most interesting and also important piece of furniture in an Eastern home. Indeed, the grinding of the millstone is the sweetest music to the Oriental; it means there is food in the home, and not famine. It is indeed an evil day when the "sound of the grinding is low" (Eccl. 12:4). Only enough corn is ground for one day's needs, so the mill is in daily use.

The peasant women are modest and wear long tobes or dresses which touch the ground as they walk. They always keep their hair covered, but when grinding at home where no man sees them, they remove the veil, uncovering the hair, and bare a greater part of the right leg. Isa. 47:2 says: "Take the millstones, and grind meal: uncover thy locks, make bare thy leg, uncover the thigh."

Jer. 25:10 says, "I will take away from thee all that would bring joy and happiness and comfort to a village. I will take from thee the voice of gladness, the voice of the bridegroom, and the voice of the bride, the sound of the millstones and the light of the candle."

"Graven on the Palms of My Hands"
(Isa. 49:16)

"Behold, I have graven thee upon the palms of my hands."

This is another Scripture reference more easily understood in the light of the East, where tattooing is very common and useful in countries where comparatively few people have learned to read or write.

Isaiah has a beautiful picture in his mind, a picture of a mother and her son, her boy far away. Neither mother nor son know one letter from another, and yet the mother longs for some token to remind her of her absent boy. She has only one means at hand and she takes advantage of that. She goes to a man who tattooes and has something pricked on the palm of her hand that will constantly remind her of the son she loves and longs to see. It will never wash off or wear away, but will remain on her palm as long as her life lasts, where she can see it as she goes about her work.

Isaiah represents Jehovah as speaking to Israel first, but to us also. "Can a woman forget her sucking child, that she should not have compassion upon the son of her body? Yea, she may forget, yet will I not forget thee. Behold, I have graven thee upon the palms of my hands."

Thou Wast Not Swaddled at All
(Ezek. 16:4)

"Thou wast not salted at all, nor swaddled at all."

Only an outcast and neglected baby would be treated like that. Back in Bible days the new babies were well rubbed with coarse salt, to "make them strong"; then their arms and legs were bound tightly to their bodies to "make them straight." They were kept bound or swaddled up to forty days.

"And Mary brought forth her firstborn son, and wrapped him in swaddling clothes, and laid him in a manger" (Luke 2:7).

A great many of the native babies are swaddled today as in Old Testament times, and as the Christ child was swaddled.

"Thou wast not salted at all, nor swaddled at all."

Weaning of a Child
(I Sam. 1:24)

Hannah brings Samuel to Eli. "And when she had weaned him, she took him up with her, . . . and brought him into the house of the Lord in Shiloh: and the child was young."

It appears strange to us to read of Samuel's mother taking her child to Eli for service in the temple as soon as she weaned him. However, in that country children, and especially boys, are not weaned until they are three, four and often even seven years of age.

So we see that Hannah did not bring a small baby to the temple for the aged prophet to take care of, but a lad of several years of age.

Lost Coin
(Luke 15:8)

"Either what woman having ten pieces of silver, if she lose one piece, doth not light a candle, and sweep the house, and seek diligently till she find it?"

When a Bethlehem woman marries, her bridegroom gives her a wedding gift of ten pieces of silver which she wears on a chain hanging from her curious helmet, with a central pendant. She prizes this gift very much and guards it carefully, because any carelessness on her part would be regarded by her husband as lack of affection and respect for him.

He could even think she had purchased a lover with the lost money and he could, and very likely would, divorce her. These coins were held sacred by the Jews and could not be taken for a debt. The wife could use this money only in case of need in widowhood.

The lost coin of Christ's parable was probably one of this chain of ten pieces of silver. We can understand the woman's concern and anxiety when she lost the silver and why she rejoiced and called in her neighbors to rejoice with her when she found it.

"And She Painted Her Face"
Making Her Eyes With Paint (Hebrew)
(II Kings 9:30)

The ladies of the Bible Lands have always had the same mode of making themselves beautiful. They "paint" or rather blacken their eyelids and brows with kohl and prolong the application in a decreasing pencil, so as to lengthen the eye in appearance to make it almond shape.

The custom of painting is very, very ancient, for painted eyes, faces, fingernails and toe nails are found on the mummies in the very oldest of the Egyptian tombs. They applied to the cheeks colored paints of different shades. The powder from which kohl is made is collected from burning almond shells, or frankincense, and is *very* black.

The powder is kept in metal containers, and is applied to the eyes by a small probe made of wood, ivory or silver, which they call *meel*, while they call the whole apparatus *mukhuly*. A very large number of paint jars of metal and alabaster of all sizes and shapes have been removed from the very oldest tombs in Egypt, so after all cosmetics are not so very modern, but are as old as the desire of the human heart to be beautiful, which means as old as the human race itself.

Painting does not appear, however, to have been by any means universal among the Hebrews. The notices of it are few; and in each instance it seems to have been unworthy of a woman of high character. Thus Jezebel "put her eyes in painting" (II Kings 9:30, margin). Jeremiah says of the harlot city, "Though thou rentest thy face with painting" (Jer. 4:30); and Ezekiel again makes it a characteristic of a harlot (Ezek. 23:40). The paint was moistened with oil, and kept in small jars made of horn.

"And she painted her face."

CHAPTER 3

GARMENTS

THE native's ordinary outfit consists of an undershirt, a long loose garment reaching to the ankles, and an outer cloak.

The material is cotton, white or dark blue, and sometimes silk for the outer cloak for the women, and wool for the men.

They wear very bright colors and much jewelry. The various styles of the outer cloak show the social rank of the wearer.

Seamless Coat
(John 19:23)

"The coat was without seam, woven from the top throughout."

In the southern part of Palestine the *abba,* or outside cloak, of the fellah is made of two strips of material joined by a seam. In the northern part of the country the abbas are made of one piece of material, woven throughout without a seam.

Many artists picture the Lord dressed in an outstanding and very fancy way, but coming from Galilee, He must have dressed as a Galilean peasant, and worn over his other garments a seamless abba or cloak such as they wore in northern Palestine.

Garment Not to Be Taken in Pledge
(Exodus 22:26, 27)

"If thou at all take thy neighbor's raiment to pledge, thou shalt deliver it unto him by that the sun goeth down: For that is his covering only, it is his garment for his skin: wherein shall he sleep?"

Retiring in a native home at night is a much more simple affair than in our country. The place where a man has been lounging around all day becomes his bed at night.

There is no furniture whatever in the tents or the guest rooms. When dusk comes, the mother spreads mats and rugs all over the floor or ground, and on these the whole family sleep; often three or four generations live in a one-room house, and they all sleep on the floor together.

When the peasant becomes sleepy, he just lies down in his clothes, wherever he happens to be at the time, — on the ground, on the sidewalk, or in the fields, it doesn't matter to him; he pulls one of the wide sleeves of his cloak over his head, wraps the cloak around his body and he is asleep. Almost always his legs and feet are bare and exposed to the weather, rain or cold or even snow, but with no apparent discomfort to him at all. Many times we have been obliged to walk out on the street because a man or boy, or perhaps several, were having a nap on the sidewalk, head covered, legs and feet bare.

It is a very common sight to see men and boys thus sleeping, often with a stone for a pillow, not under the head, as we have our pillows, but under the neck.

Even today the giving of a small article as a pledge of security is very common. Still the taking of a coat or cloak for a pledge is considered most unkind, as it deprives the owner of his only night covering.

This commandment, given so long ago to a people like the peasants of today, is still religiously kept, — a proof of how very little the customs of the Bible Lands have changed since Old Testament days.

"If thou take thy neighbor's raiment to pledge, thou shalt deliver it to him before the sun goes down."

Sackcloth
(Rev. 6:12)

"And the sun became black as sackcloth of hair."

Sackcloth is a very heavy, coarse, dark colored cloth of goat's hair. It is worn as a sign of mourning, next to the skin. Esther 4:1 says that "Mordecai rent his clothes, and put on sackcloth with ashes . . . and cried with a bitter cry."

"Rend your clothes, and gird you with sackcloth, and mourn" (II Sam. 3:31) .

Conversely, the putting off of sackcloth was, and is, a symbol of joy, of thanksgiving for deliverance from an intolerable position or condition; it celebrated a changing of affliction by one's enemies to the casting off of the yoke of bondage (Psalm 30:11) .

"They Enlarge the Borders of Their Garments"
(Matt. 23:5)

There are *zizith* or fringes at each corner, and those the Jews reverently kiss. Numbers 15:38: "Speak unto the children of Israel, and bid them that they make them fringes in the borders of their garments throughout their generations, and that they put upon the fringes of the borders a ribband of blue.

In Bible days this robe was the distinctive garment worn by the Jews, but during the Maccabean persecution the Jews were so easily distinguished by their dress that, as a measure of safety, they were allowed by Jewish leaders to wear the fringe on an inner robe, only during the hour of prayer. This they continue to do to the present day. They call it now a "prayer shawl."

Probably Christ, as a strict Jew, wore the fringes on an outer garment. The "hem of his garment" was the zizith (Luke 8:44). The woman came behind Him, and touched the border or fringe of his garment.

The *talith* is generally a gift to a son by his mother when he is made "Son of the Law" (Bar-Mitzvah ceremony); and by a bride to her bridegroom.

Women never wear a talith, as they are not obliged to pray. A talith is worn by a Jew over his head or shoulders while praying. It is shaped like a shawl or a scarf now, but in Bible days it was a man's upper garment. Blue stripes are woven into the white at each end.

"And put upon the fringe at the borders a ribband of blue."

Coat of Many Colours
(Gen. 37:3)

"Now Israel loved Joseph more than all his children, because he was the son of his old age: and he made him a coat of many colours."

In the Authorized Version of the Bible you find that the word "many" is in italics, always indicating that it was not in the original, and we also notice that the word translated "colours" is given in the margin as "pieces."

In the margin of the Revised Version we find this "a long garment with sleeves." Very likely the translators puzzled as to why Jacob should give his son a coat with pieces or a long garment with sleeves as a mark of favor, decided that it surely must have been a very wonderful brilliant kind of garment, more beautiful than the other sons had, so they missed the whole meaning of Joseph's gift from his father. It also appeared that the older brothers were very childish men, aroused by jealousy because Joseph had been given a very handsome coat.

This "coat of many colours," so called, was a plain long white shirt, the *kamise,* or undergarment of the desert ranger. In nearly all of those garments the sleeves were of moderate size, but the Bedouin told us that only two people in each whole tribe are allowed the privilege of the extremely long pointed sleeve — the Sheikh of the tribe and the man whom he had chosen as his heir.

So the wrath of the elder brothers was not an outburst of childish anger. It represented a very deep-seated hurt of mature men whose claim to succession to the leadership of their tribe had been set aside for their younger brother.

However, we must see Jacob's viewpoint and feeling about it, too. Jacob had been fearfully deceived by his father-in-law when, after serving seven years for Rachel, the woman he loved, he was given Leah for his wife instead. Then he served seven years more for Rachel. Had Jacob married Rachel as he desired, her son would have been Jacob's heir.

As it was, Leah's sons were born first, but Jacob very much desired that his wife Rachel's son, Joseph, should be heir as he should have been. Therefore, Jacob makes, or has made, the garment with the long sleeves to be worn by his heir and gives it to Joseph.

"And Jacob made him a coat with long sleeves."

"Now We See Through a Glass Darkly"
(I Cor. 13:12)

After seeing the mirrors of the Bible days, we understand the meaning of these words of the apostle Paul.

The word *glass* was never in the original, but *mirror.* When the Hebrews left Egypt, they brought with them their mirrors, which were made of bronze, copper alloyed with tin, the brass of the Bible. They were so well made that they had a wonderful lustre.

Upper Left

Tourists in Boaz' field

Center Left

A lodge in a garden of cucumbers. Where the laborer rests during harvest

Lower Left

Pile of witness stones.

Upper Right

"Thy neighbor's landmark." The small pile of stones which separates one man's field from his neighbor's.

Center Right

Watch tower near Bethlehem.

Lower Right

"A cottage in a vineyard," where the peasant finds shelter from the sun during harvest

A great many mirrors found in tombs at Thebes, although buried in the earth for many centuries, have been cleaned and polished until they again give a fairly clear reflection. The mirrors were always round, with a metal handle.

How illuminating is the account given us of the sacrifice of the children of Israel giving their mirrors, which were melted and used as the metal for the production of the laver in the court of the Tabernacle.

It was natural to translate "mirror" as "glass," but the spade has shown us that all the mirrors of Bible days were metal.

"Now we see through or by means of a mirror, darkly, but then face to face."

"A Good Name is Better Than Precious Ointment"
(Eccl. 7:1)

We can scarcely understand the value put upon perfumes and ointments by the Eastern people, and their enjoyment of the perfumes, especially at their feasts of all kinds. Many of them were fearfully expensive. They kept their perfumes in very precious vases and jars of alabaster and glass and metal.

Perfumes are so much used in Eastern countries that the omission of them means that one is in mourning. The perfumes mentioned in the Bible were applied in various ways. Often the people wore perfumes about their persons; sometimes they were used in the way of fumigation; sometimes the perfume was extracted and mixed with oil, and used afterward as ointment; and sometimes the perfume was kept in bottles, which were fastened to the girdle, — but the Word told them that a good name was even better than that.

Veil

The Eastern or original veil may be anything from a square yard to three or four square yards in dimension.

It is usually of cotton material, and is worn down the back, not necessarily covering the face. The veil is useful in many ways, especially for carrying things in. Ruth would have no difficulty in carrying sir measures of barley presented to her by Boaz.

A veil is always used at a wedding ceremony to cover the face of the bride. Even the Bedouin women, who never cover their faces on ordinary occasions, have their brides' faces covered, and the removing of the veil is the great point in the wedding ceremony. The bridegroom, after walking round the bride three times, removes the veil from her face and throws it over his shoulder. It is a proclamation to all that the government of his bride rests upon him. How very wonderfully this ceremony is brought to notice in the prophecy referring to our Lord, "the government shall be upon his shoulder" (Isa. 9:6) —Christ in glory reigning with His bride, the Church.

Saul Lay Sleeping
(I Sam. 26:7)

The sheikh's tent was always distinguished from all other tents by a tall spear standing upright in the ground in front of the tent. It was customary, when a party went out on an excursion to rob or for war, that at night the place where the chief slept was designated by a spear. So Saul, lying asleep, had his spear stuck in the ground at his head and the people lay round about him.

This whole scene is truly Oriental, even to the deep sleep into which the whole party had fallen. Then the cruse of water at Saul's head agrees with the customs of the people of that day. It is a hot, dry country and the people need a drink in the night, and the quantity that an Arab can drink is enormous.

We see Saul and his party asleep in a shady valley, after the weariness of a hot day. David, from the hillside, marks the spot where the king slumbers, creeps carefully down and stands over his persecutor. Abishai pleads with David to be allowed to strike him once, just once; but David forbade him, and, taking the cruse of water and the spear, he ascends to the top of the hill and then cried out to Abner, Saul's body guard. What a sensation must have gone through the camp as David's voice rings from the hill-top!

"Art not thou a valiant man? and who is like thee in Israel? . . . As the Lord liveth, ye are worthy to die, because ye have not kept your master, the Lord's anointed. And now see where the king's spear is and the cruse of water that was at his bolster." (I Sam. 26:15).

CHAPTER 4

CLOTHING AND JEWELS

"Her Clothing Is Silk and Purple"
(Prov. 31:22)

"SHE maketh herself coverings of tapestry; her clothing is silk and purple."

King Lemuel tells us that all the household of a virtuous woman "are clothed with scarlet." Girls and women will spend all their spare time making beautiful garments, embroidered and spangled with gold, silver, and flowers.

In several homes I visited, the women with great pride showed me their wardrobe of from a dozen to twenty very heavy outer garments, all hand work. Some of them were made before their marriage, some belonged to the mother or even to the grandmother. They were only worn on great festivals, like Christmas or Easter, when they just sit in state to receive their friends, and pass around coffee and pipes. One can scarcely understand *why* so many fine garments, when you consider their humble occupations; for, daily, except on these big occasions, you find them sweeping out the kitchen, boiling the pot, collecting thorns for the fire, and doing all the hard work of the home and the field too, or going to market to sell the vegetables they have raised.

The woman eats her meals after her husband and his friends have finished, just sitting on the ground with her small children around her, outside the room where the men had their meal and are now smoking and talking.

She wears her hair in a large number of braids, which hang down the whole length of her back, with money tied to the end of each braid, which together with what she wears on her forehead would be worth fifty dollars or more. All through the long braids you would see charms and evil eye beads.

"She Took a Veil and Covered Herself"
(Gen. 24:65)

"When Rebekah saw Isaac in the field, she took a veil and covered herself."

The veil is a very important and indispensable article in the East and has been so since the very earliest times. The women have at least four kinds of veils; two kinds for the home and two different kinds for the street.

The first is made like a kerchief, falling on the back of the wearer just as an ornament. The second passes under the chin and falls over the chest. The third is the white veil, which covers the whole body, nearly. The fourth is a sort of handkerchief, which is worn to cover the face.

For a woman to be seen on the street without a veil would be a calamity.

In ancient times the veil was the most important part of an Eastern woman's dress — her chief concern was always to hide her face. Only the Christian women go unveiled today.

"Mine Horn Is Exalted in the Lord"
(I Sam. 2:1)

This was Hannah's triumphant cry.

Job, stripped of all his glory, could say, "I have defiled my horns in the dust."

The horn was an ornament worn on the head. It was an emblem of power and authority, and the habit of wearing a horn, though not so common, has not yet entirely disappeared.

In addition to the various trinkets worn on the head, neck and arms, the Syrian women wear a hollow horn, made of copper or silver. It is tapering and varies from fifteen to twenty inches in length. It cannot be a very comfortable adornment pressing against the forehead. It is held in place by straps, and over the horn is thrown a veil of white muslin, which can be drawn over the face for concealment. The horns worn by the men were shorter. This ornament is mentioned in II Sam. 22:3; I Kings 22:11; Psalm 75:5, and other places.

"With Their Loins Girded"
(Exodus 12:11)

Another very important part of the Eastern costume is the girdle, which is a long piece of cloth like a shawl, folded around the waist or loins. It is useful in keeping in order the long loose robes worn in those countries. Christ frequently alludes to the uses of the girdle, and bids His people to be ready, waiting for their Lord; having their loins girded and not to sit in idleness with loose and disordered garments. These girdles are still worn by both men and women, some are worsted, some silk, and the Bedouin men often wear leather girdles.

"Round Tires Like the Moon"
(Isa. 3:16-24)

The Old Testament abounds with references to such ornaments and even the style of them has scarcely changed. Chains and bracelets and earrings, and headbands, and tinkling ornaments for the feet and "round tires like the moon" of silver or gold to place on the head under the veil, and the nose-rings are as fashionable today as ever. The tire is a kind of round cap of gold or silver, beaten very thin and hung all around with money and precious stones. The women are exceedingly proud of these "tires."

A Gold Chain About Joseph's Neck
(Gen. 41:42)

Pharaoh put a gold chain about Joseph's neck at the time of Joseph's exaltation. Bracelets and chains are often mentioned in the Bible. Eliezer gave Rachel bracelets that weighed ten shekels. The Jewish women are still addicted to wearing heavy bracelets. But bracelets and chains were worn by men of noble birth and officials of high rank. Belshazzar placed a gold chain around the neck of Daniel. Saul had a bracelet around his arm. The same kinds of chains and bracelets can be found on arms and around necks today in the Land of the Bible.

"I Put a Jewel on Thy Nose"
(Isa. 3:21)

Many of the women in parts of the Bible Lands still wear rings in the left nostril, which is bored low down in the center. These rings are usually of gold with pearls or rubies placed in the ring.

The men formerly wore nose rings. In Gen. 24:22, "I put the earring upon her face," the correct translation is, "I put a jewel on her nose."

"Thy Signet, and Thy Bracelets, and Thy Staff"
(Gen. 38:18)

The articles most appropriate to a patriarch were, "a staff, a signet-ring, and bracelets." Thus when Judah asked Tamar what pledge she desired from him, she replied, "Thy

signet, and thy bracelets, and thy staff that is in thine hand."
The ring was engraved with the name of the owner or with
some emblem.

Both sexes wore rings, both for ornament and use. The
one for use had seals or signets, and are much used today
where the custom of sealing every document still prevails.
A document without a seal would not be legal. A mer-
chant's letters and bills must be sealed.

The modern Egyptians wear the seal-ring on the little
finger of the right hand. The ring is usually silver, with a
carnelian or other stone, upon which is engraved the owner's name.

"Pharaoh took off his ring from his hand, and put it on
Joseph's hand." "The king took his ring and gave it to
Mordecai." Job 38:14, "It is turned as clay to the seal." In
Egypt the granary doors were kept sealed, but not with
wax. The inspectors put the seal of their rings upon a
handful of clay and covered the lock.

The ring is still an emblem of authority in Egypt, Tur-
key, Persia, and other parts of the East. When Pharaoh
placed his ring upon Joseph's hand, it meant delegated
power, and Pharaoh could have conferred no greater honor.

Ornaments of the Feet and Legs

"In that day the Lord will take away the bravery of their
tinkling ornaments about their feet . . . and the ornaments
of their legs."

Anklets and stride-chains are unknown in our country,
but not in the Bible Lands. The effect of the stride chain
was to shorten the step, and the anklet was covered with
bells. The daughters of Zion are described as "walking and
mincing as they go, and making a tinkling with their feet"
Isa. 3:16.

Arab ladies are extravagantly fond of silver and gold ornaments and they also wear silver money around the forehead, suspended from the neck, and attached to the back.

The jewels can never be taken for the husband's debts. A poor man may go to jail for a few piasters (one piaster is five cents) while thousands glitter on the dress of his wife. Often the husband purposely gives his wife the money to escape liability for just debts.

Beds and Bedchambers
(Matt. 9:6)

The bed of Bible Lands is not at all like the piece of furniture we are accustomed to in our homes; it is like a quilt. The Eastern bed is not a bed-stead, but a thick mat, very easily rolled up and carried under the arm.

The Bible Lands bedrooms are not rooms kept for sleeping at all, they are merely recesses in the ordinary family room, in which the folded-up mats or quilts are placed during the day. It was in one of these recesses in the wall made to hold the mats to sleep on that the little king Joash, was hidden by his aunt Jehosheba (II Kings 11:2). "But Jehosheba, the daughter of King Joram, . . . took Joash, the son of Ahaziah, and stole him from among the king's sons which were slain; and they hid him, even him and his nurse, in the bedchamber from Athaliah, so that he was not slain." Sometimes the word translated "bed" in English refers to the Eastern *deewan* or couch, quite another thing from the mat or quilt of Matthew 9:6, where Christ said to the man he healed, "Arise, take up thy bed, and go into thine house."

We are too apt to get a very wrong impression of the incident in Esther 7:8, from the use of our English word "bed." Here in this Scripture, the word "bed" merely means the couch or deewan on which the queen was sitting. Very likely it was a raised stone platform built against the wall, as you see in many homes even today. The word "pillow" too, is liable to give an incorrect idea. When Jacob used a stone for a pillow, he was doing what he did every day and what others did.

"My Children Are With Me in Bed"
(Luke 11:7)

"Trouble me not; the door is now shut, and my children are with me in bed; I cannot rise and give thee bread."

The village home has only one room, and here all the family sleep. Very often three or even four generations and perhaps widowed sisters and aunts, live together in one house. The house is divided into two parts, one part raised a few feet above the rest. This highest part is used by the family for a kitchen, dining room and living room by day, and a bedroom at night.

The lower part is the room for the animals. In the summer they sleep in the open, but the rest of the year, when night comes the man puts the animals in the house with the family. They tell you that the breath of the animals helps to keep the family warm. At night you see the ox and a donkey or two, a few goats and perhaps a dog, all sleeping below the family.

When dark comes, because they go to bed soon after sunset, the people spread their mats or quilts on the floor, and all living in the house lie down in their clothes together and sleep.

For the father to rise to attend to the needs of a neighbor would awaken the whole household, so the man had a far better excuse than we might at first think he had.

"Israel Bowed Himself Upon the Bed's Head"
(Gen. 47:31)

Then in Hebrews 11:21 we read, "leaning upon the top of his staff." Hebrews gives the correct rendering. There are two words in Hebrew of which the consonants are exactly the same. Up to the sixth century no vowels or vowel points appear in Hebrew usage, and the context alone decided which of the two words of similar consonants was intended by the writer. In this Scripture there is apparent confusion between two Hebrew words: *mittah,* place of reclining, and *mattah,* staff. The staff was the symbol of patriarchal authority, and, leaning upon it, oaths were made or solemn injunctions given. Compare the practice of Bishops giving their benediction leaning on the Pastoral Staff. Jacob's bed was probably the ordinary bed of the desert wanderer, the *ilhaf,* a mere mat or thick quilt.

"A Cottage in a Vineyard, a Lodge in a Garden of Cucumbers"

(Isaiah 1:8)

We can understand a cottage in a garden in our country. To us appears a small but substantial house, but what it really happens to mean is a booth lightly constructed of brushwood, in which the farmer and his family live during harvest time, where they are laboring. The Feast of Booths or Tabernacles was celebrated, and is now, in just such structures or cottages. The farmer may live a distance from his farm or garden, so in the time of harvest he builds a light structure in which they all live to protect the harvest from thieves.

"A lodge in a garden" was something similar, but flimsier in construction. It refers to the rude shelter which the laborer builds for himself in a field where he is hired.

Harvest is past and the people return to their homes, but these structures, cottage and lodge, are never removed, but left to fall apart. The heavy rains of winter beat upon them, the fierce winds tear them in pieces, and these tattered parts present a sorry spectacle of ruin, which is a good picture of a people whom God, grieved by their rejection of His love, has left to themselves. "The daughter of Zion is left as a cottage in a vineyard, as a lodge in a garden of cucumbers."

"A Lamp in Jerusalem"
(I Kings 15:4)

A native in the Bible Lands will not sleep in a dark room. However poor he may be, he absolutely must have some light.

To them it is the symbol of the supremacy of good over evil, the triumph of life over death.

An Eastern home is never in darkness except for one of two reasons. Either the inmates of the home are dead, or the house is deserted. The many references to lamps are symbolic of the continuance of a family. Job says (Job 18:5, 6), "the light of the wicked shall be put out, and the spark of his fire shall not shine. The light shall be dark in his tabernacle, and his candle shall be put out with him."

We see in Proverbs 13:9, "The light of the righteous rejoiceth: but the lamp of the wicked shall be put out."

"I Will Pour Water on Him That is Thirsty"
(Isaiah 44:3)

An Easterner in drinking water, never touches the earthen water-jar to his lips. He tilts back his head, holds the vessel high above him, pours a stream of water down into his mouth, and — he never appears to swallow; the water just runs down his throat and he never spills it on his face or clothes. "I will pour water on him that is thirsty."

Broken Sherd
(Isaiah 30:14)

"A sherd to take fire from the hearth, or to take water withal out of the pit."

This picture, which means little or nothing to our minds, was full of beauty to those who first heard it spoken. Pitchers and jars of earthenware are the usual means of carrying water from the well to the home. These jars are very easily broken. A woman stumbles or falls on her way to the well, the vessel crashes from her head to the ground and there lies in pieces. Frugality is one of the Eastern woman's virtues. Even these broken pieces of pottery (sherds) may be turned to service. She selects two of the largest: one she places by the side of the well or water pit; the other she takes home and places beneath the hearth. The piece by the well side will serve some day for the thirsty traveler to stoop down and scoop up the cool waters out of the pit. The sherd by the hearth will be used to carry glowing embers to light another fire, perhaps in a neighbor's home.

Now we see the full vividness and force of Isaiah's analogy, which depicts the utter ruin of rebellious and faithless Israel: "As a potter's vessel that is broken in pieces he shall not spare: so that there shall not be found in the bursting of it a sherd to take fire from the hearth, or water withal out of the pit."

Rings

(Isa. 3:21)

When Pharaoh committed the government of Egypt to Joseph, he took his ring from his finger and gave it to Joseph. (Gen. 41:42) After the victory of the Israelites over the Midianites, they offered to the Lord the rings, the bracelets, and the golden necklaces, taken from the enemy (Num. 31:50). St. James (James 2:2) distinguishes a man of wealth and dignity by the ring of gold on his finger (Luke 15:22). The ring was used chiefly to seal with; and the Scripture generally assigns it to princes and great persons — as the king of Egypt, Joseph, Ahaz, Jezebel, and others.

The patents and orders of these princes were sealed with their rings or signets, an impression from which was their confirmation. The ring was one mark of sovereign authority. Pharaoh gave his ring to Joseph, as a token of authority."

"I Will Make Thee As a Signet"
(Haggai 2:23)

In that day . . . O Zerubbabel . . . I will make thee as a signet" (seal ring). The meaning is evident from the importance of the signet ring in the eyes of the Oriental, who is accustomed if he owns a ring to carry it constantly with him, and to care for it as one of his most prized and valuable possessions. The signet being an emblem of authority, was used to stamp documents and other legal articles. Indeed, without being stamped by a signet, no document was considered authentic.

"I will make thee as a signet."

CHAPTER 5

PEASANT MEN

"Take It for Nothing"
(Gen. 23:11-16)

WHEN Ephron the Hittite offered the field to Abraham as a burying place for Sarah, he said, "I give it thee"; but, doubtless, with just as much thought of doing so as the Arab dealers of today, when they say, "Take it for nothing." And the Hittite finally charged Abraham far more than the land was worth.

Today, in the Eastern lands, when a customer prices an article, the dealer will usually reply, "Take it for nothing, I shall be happy to make you a present of it." But by this they mean that they expect a present in return, of very much greater value.

If you desire to buy anything, the best way is to push it to one side and seem indifferent about it. Then the seller is almost sure to name a price somewhat near an honest value. They always keep the best goods in the background, and only bring them out when they see they cannot sell you the inferior ones.

Gen. 23:15: "And the Hittite said to Abraham, The land is worth four hundred shekels of silver; what is that betwixt thee and me? bury thy dead, I will give it thee."

"Go to the Ant, Thou Sluggard"
(Prov. 6:6-11)

Laziness appears to have been a very prevalent vice in these countries from days of old. Solomon appears to have more to say about this subject than any other. His rebuke of the sluggard drawn from the habits of the ant is very suggestive. Solomon so intensely disliked laziness, that he expressed his dislike of it in many ways. "The slothful man roasteth not that which he took in hunting." The most good-for-nothing creature may be roused by the excitement of the hunt, but is too indolent to roast the game afterwards. "The soul of the sluggard desireth, but hath nothing." He coveteth greedily all day, but his hands refuse to labour.

"He will not plow by reason of the cold," is true today. Plowing and sowing cannot be carried on until the winter rains commence, therefore he neglects to sow his fields.

We have known farmers go out to sow and plow, but the rain and cold proved to be more than they cared for, so they retreat into their mud huts, kindle a fire, and doze away the time by the side of it. Nor can you rouse him, — as Solomon said, "A little more sleep, a little more folding of the hands."

It is said that these lazy men will not turn over on their pillow, even if muddy water is leaking from the roof into their eyes.

Proverbs, the twenty-fourth chapter, is a perfect description of the poor fellaheen today. "I went by the field of the slothful, — and, lo, it was all grown over with thorns, and nettles had covered the face thereof, and the stone wall was broken down." And the owners are too indolent to do anything about it.

Solomon surely knew the peasants of his day — and of these days too. The peasant men desire to do nothing but smoke, sleep and gossip. The women do the work and carry the burdens, mostly.

"Go to the ant, thou sluggard" — and learn her secrets of life.

"They Make Broad Their Phylacteries"
(Matt. 23:5)

"All their works they do for to be seen of men: they make broad their phylacteries, and enlarge the borders of their garments."

In Exodus 13:9, 10, 16; Deut. 6:4-9; 11:18-21, we find the Israelites commanded to bind the law upon their heads and on their hands, a reminder that they must live holy lives. As a symbolic witness of this the orthodox Jew even todays binds small leather boxes on his forehead and arm. These are cubic in shape, made of leather specially prepared from the skin of a clean animal. The one for the forehead has on the outside the Hebrew letter *shin,* the initial of Shaddai — Almighty. Inside it is divided into four compartments, each of which contains a piece of parchment, inscribed with one of the above passages from the Pentateuch. The phylactery for the arm has only one compartment, and has all those passages of Scripture on a small scroll inserted.

An expert prepares these phylacteries, and the very slightest mistake from the rules renders them worthless. They are fastened to the forehead and arm with leather straps with knots tied in a certain pattern.

The young Hebrew wears these for the first time when he comes to the age of Bar-Mitzvah, twelve or thirteen years old. He then goes through a ceremony, and is considered a man, responsible for himself.

Jesus at the age of twelve must have gone through this ceremony, and after this He was found in the temple hearing the doctors and asking them questions.

The wearing of phylacteries externally was too often a symbol with no reality back of it, and Christ rebuked the Jews for this outward show. "All their works they do to be seen of men," was what Jesus said to them.

"The Sabbath Was Made for Man"
(Mark 2:27)

Christ said, "The sabbath was made for man and not man for the sabbath."

The weekly day of rest was one of God's beautiful plans for man's mental and physical rest from labor, and a day to especially cultivate his spiritual nature, a day for fellowship with God. It began at sunset on Friday and ended at sunset on Saturday. When Christ was on earth, man had a tendency to observe the sabbath in letter rather than in spirit. However, even then it had its noble side. The Jew dressed himself in his festal garments: he lighted his sabbath lamp; the table was spread with special food and the men all went to the synagogue. The work was done the day before so that no work that could be avoided was done on the sabbath. It was a beautiful day of worship and rest. Then the rabbis feared that the day would not be properly observed, so they made laws which in course of time so completely destroyed the purpose of the day, that to keep all these laws that the rabbis had made, became very much harder and more exacting than the labor of the working day. Thus was God's beautiful day for meditation, worship and rest brought to nought.

One can scarcely believe that leaders could make such absurd regulations, a few of which are: The greatest burden a person might carry on the sabbath day must be less than the weight of a dried fig. They must not begin anything new just before the sabbath, lest the sabbath should find one in the midst of the task. A scribe must not carry his pen, or a tailor a needle on the sabbath.

A woman was not allowed to have a pin in her clothing, she was not allowed to look in a mirror, because she might see a white hair and be tempted to remove it, which would be labor. The rabbis forbade them to cut their nails, and many, many other absurd regulations could be mentioned which made the sabbath a very hard and unhappy day.

It had become a day of form and so lacked spiritual significance. Back of all these absurd rules there was a genuine piety and a real desire to observe the sabbath day as God had planned it.

This attitude toward the sabbath was very distasteful to the Son of God, because for Him all of God's laws were necessary for man's highest good, and were made to meet a real need.

The sabbath was made for man, not only for the physical man, but for the most important part of him, the spiritual.

"A Writer's Inkhorn by His Side"
(Ezek. 9:2)

"And one man among them was clothed with linen, with a writer's inkhorn by his side." This is a description of the scribe as you see him today in Bible Lands and as he appeared in Bible days.

Customs have changed so little in many ways since Ezekiel lived there. Very few people can read or write yet, so the scribe is needed and is a very important person in a city or town. Indeed in many villages he may be the only person who can read or write a letter.

The scribe carries an inkhorn in his girdle or leather belt. The inkhorn is usually about ten inches long by two inches wide, made of wood or metal. It is really a long tube and holds the wooden pens. In the upper end of this case the inkstand is attached.

The ink is made of powdered charcoal, lampblack, or soot, mixed with gum and water. It is exceedingly black and would never fade out, but could very easily be washed off the parchment with water.

You see today the scribes writing letters for people or reading a letter for them, near the gates, or on street corners.

"He Wrote on the Ground"
(John 8:6)

"Jesus stooped down, and with his finger wrote on the ground."

"This story of Jesus writing in the sand appears picturesque, unusual. Instead, it was the common, universal habit or practice. You visit a native camp or village today and you will see Bedouins sitting idle, scribbling words or sentences with their finger or a camel-wand. Often when they desire to describe something to you they will draw the whole plan in the sand with their finger. Sometimes in bargaining for sheep or goats all the computations will be made by writing in the sand. It has always been and is today a common practice.

"Jesus stooped down, and with his finger wrote on the ground."

A White Stone
(Rev. 2:17)

"I will give him a white stone." This Scripture makes one think of another custom. If a man sins against a young woman of his tribe or of another tribe, he will be put to death. However, sometimes the people accept "blood" money and the culprit goes free. Always afterwards he lives in a white tent, or rides a white camel, and has a large white stone in front of his tent.

These are to show that no one has any right to harm him; he is forgiven; the price is paid and it is with him now as though he had never committed the sin.

"I will give him a white stone."

Forgiveness, vindication, a proof of forgiveness shown by the white stone.

Little Children
(II Kings 2:23)

As Elisha went up to Bethel "there came forth little children out of the city, and mocked him."

The Hebrew word here does not mean little children, any more than does the word used by the Lord in John 21:5. "Then Jesus said unto them, Children, have ye any meat?" Both terms have a general meaning. The "children" who mocked Elisha and were punished so severely, were no doubt young men.

"Hands of the Masters"
(Psalm 123:2)

"As the eyes of servants look unto their masters, and the eyes of a maiden unto the hand of her mistress: so our eyes wait upon the Lord our God."

In Palestine a servant is summoned, not by calling, but by clapping the hands, and, to show what you require of them, you gesture, but do not speak a word.

In a country where life is simple, this is much easier than in our part of the world. However, even there the servant must watch closely or he or she will fail in service.

What a beautiful illustration of the relationship which should exist between the Lord and His servants!

"Our eyes wait upon the Lord our God."

"Kicking Against the Pricks"
(Acts 26:14)

"It is hard for thee to kick against the pricks."

The plowman in Bible Lands carries in his hand a long pole or goad, with a sharp metal point or prick on one end of the pole and at the other there is a flat piece of iron which is used to clean the plowshare. Quite often the young ox, probably not well broken in, will kick, because he does not like his work. The plowman then holds the pole or goad in such a position that when the ox kicks again, he will kick against that prick or sharp point, and thus the animal will learn it doesn't pay.

Paul, kicking against the plan of God, learned his mistake. "Saul, Saul, why persecutest thou me? It is hard for thee to kick against the pricks."

"Iniquities Like a Heavy Burden
(Psalm 38:4)

One of the first things we noticed in Palestine, and we could scarcely believe our eyes, was the enormous loads carried by the porter or *atal*. You can scarcely understand unless you have seen these burdens yourself.

We have several times seen a single porter carry an ordinary piano on his back for quite a distance. His piled up burden very often extends far beyond his head.

After the burden has been placed on the porter's back, he cannot easily lay it down until he has reached his destination. When he becomes desperately weary and must have a little rest, he calls a wayfarer, and the latter just stoops down under the load for a few minutes, takes the weight of the burden from the weary porter, and gives him a short rest. This is what Gal. 6:2, "Bear ye one another's burdens," means.

In the same chapter and the fifth verse we read, "for every man shall bear his own burden." That sounds like a contradiction, but not so. In our Greek Testament in verse two we have the word *baros,* meaning the very heavy burden like the porter carries; in verse five we have this word, *phortion,* the light burden that any person might carry in his hand.

The Word of God is telling us that Christians must be ready to get under another's heavy load and give him a little rest, he must not throw his own lawful burdens upon others, he must carry the light ones alone.

"I Cast Out My Shoe"
(Psalm 60:8; 108:9)

"Over Edom will I cast out my shoe."

The shoe, like a dog, is considered unclean. In Palestine houses there is always a threshold called the *mastaby,* where the people of the house and all guests remove their shoes and enter barefooted. Shoes are never worn in a mosque or in well-to-do homes where they have rugs over the floors. Shoes are never spoken of with respect, but in terms of very great disrespect.

The angel of the Lord said to Moses (Exodus 3:5), "Draw not nigh hither: put off thy shoes from off thy feet, for the place whereon thou standest is holy ground."

In Joshua 5:15, "And the captain of the Lord's host said unto Joshua, Loose thy shoe from off thy foot; for the place whereon thou standest is holy."

David, speaking by inspiration, was deriding Edom and said, "Upon Edom will I throw my shoe." David, to humble Edom, considers that country as an equal only to the mastaby or place near the door used for the purpose of casting unclean shoes. The shoe in Bible days was always associated with everything you could think of that was low, filthy, and contemptible. It was only made and worn to protect the feet from the filth and vile things over which the person had to walk.

To unloose the shoe was the work of a slave. John the Baptist said that he was not worthy to unloose the shoes of Christ.

We see more clearly what the expression of Amos meant when he said that the rulers and oppressors had "sold . . . the poor for a pair of shoes" (Amos 2:6; 8:6). "To cast the shoe upon" anyone meant to degrade and humble him to the very limit.

"Over Edom will I cast out my shoe."

"As Trees Walking"
(Mark 8:24)

What a queer sight it was at first to us to see men, women and animals walking along the road with such huge loads of brushwood, thorn bushes, or branches that you just couldn't see what was carrying it. If it was a donkey all you could see was the lower part of four small legs.

The half-restored sight of the man who had been blind prevented him from seeing clearly between the branches and the animal that carried them, but he remembered the days when he had his sight, and he knew what these walking trees really were.

Redemption of the Purchased Possession
(Eph. 1:13, 14)

"Ye are sealed with that Holy Spirit of promise until . . . the redemption of the purchased possession."

The seal is a large wooden instrument, twenty inches or longer and has the symbol of the owner engraved upon it. When a man goes to the open market and makes a purchase of a large amount of grain lying in a big heap, he very carefully impresses the grain on all sides with his seal. In that way he makes it impossible for anyone to steal his grain without breaking his symbol and thus protects his purchase until he returns to remove it to his own house or barn.

The Book says that is what God does for His purchased possession, His redeemed ones, until He removes them to the Owner's home. "After that ye believed, ye were sealed with that Holy Ghost of promise, which is the earnest (or pledge) of our inheritance until the redemption of the purchased possession, unto the praise of his glory."

"They Comfort Me"
(Psalm 23:4)

The heavy clubs carried by the shepherds are a means of defense, for the shepherd never knows what he may meet. They are the clubs mentioned in the Shepherd Psalm.

Where would the "comfort" come in? The weight of these clubs would not feel comfortable. The watchful shepherd is always guarding his sheep that they may not be injured or killed by wild animals.

If a wild animal approaches, the shepherd comes and with all the strength he has, he brings the heavy rod down upon the enemy of his sheep and they are saved.

Then, sometimes the sheep or the little lambs are caught in the thorns or bushes or they may fall into a deep hole. The shepherd then takes his staff and tenderly lifts the lamb out of its difficulty.

He also leans on the staff when walking over rough, stony paths.

"Thy rod and thy staff, they comfort me."

"A Bruised Reed"
(Isa. 42:3)

"A bruised reed shall he not break, and the smoking flax shall he not quench."

The shepherd spends much time alone with his sheep in desert solitudes; and his reed pipe, a frail little instrument of two reeds bound together, hollowed out and with holes on the side, helps to pass the hours cheerfully. He learns to play many little tunes on it. It is very easily broken and if it falls and is crushed by a careless foot, its music is stilled. It is of almost no value, a new one could easily be made and the bruised pipe left by the wayside to rot.

But the shepherd appears to have a sentimental feeling about it; he will not let it go, not at all. He picks up the crushed reed, and so tenderly repairs it, binding up its broken parts, until once more he draws from it the music he dearly loves. "A bruised reed shall he not break."

What a picture of the sinner, bruised and broken by sin, of no apparent value, lying by the wayside; and then God's love and concern and His desire to restore the broken life.

"The smoking flax shall he not quench." Here in this Scripture we see a little clay lamp, with its wick floating in an hour's supply of olive oil. The oil has burned out, the wick smokes. We would probably say, "Throw it out, get a fresh wick; this one smokes and it is of no value." But the owner does not agree to that, "The old will do, all that is needed is oil, then the wick will burn as brightly as ever."

That is just what God does, with His grace — restores when the light is almost out.

"The smoking flax will he not quench."

White Asses
(Judges 5:10)

"Ye that ride on white asses, ye that sit in judgment."

Palestinians acquainted with the law, religious or secular,—in other words, rabbis and lawyers—usually select the white ass for their journeys in preference to the ordinary donkey or horse, as it is much more impressive in looks and more sure footed.

"Ye that rid on white asses."

CHAPTER 6

HOME LIFE

"Sit Down in the Lowest Seat"
(Luke 14:10)

"WHEN thou art bidden to a feast, go and sit down in the lowest seat."

As we enter the Upper Room where the feast is, we see rugs over the floor and divans or seats like benches all around the walls of the room. The seats nearest the door are very low, just small mattresses or pillows on the floor; the next will be a bit higher; and the ones at the wall just opposite the door where you enter so high that your feet could not reach the floor.

All sit with the feet crossed under them. When a guest arrives he knocks at the door, and a voice from within the rooms calls out, "Who is it?" The person outside replies, "It is I," but gives no name. If the voice is recognized, the door will be opened; if not, it will remain closed.

This custom reminds us of Acts 12:13, 14, "And as Peter knocked at the gate, a damsel came to hearken, named Rhoda. And when she knew Peter's voice, she opened not the gate for gladness."

At a feast a servant or a son or younger brother shows the guest to the upper room. If the guest is polite, he will seat himself on the lowest seat, and await the arrival of the householder. When the host arrives and finds his guest on the lowest seat, he will compel him to move to a higher one. The custom of the East gives the highest seats to older persons and those of high rank. The relatives, youths, and those of lower standing sit in the lower seats.

Jesus said, "When thou art bidden to a feast, sit down in the lowest seat; that when he that bade thee cometh, he may say to thee, Friend, go up higher."

"Oh That I Had a Lodging Place"
(Jer. 9:2)

Jeremiah says, "Oh that I had in the wilderness a *lodging place* of wayfaring men."

Genesis 42:27 says, "as one of them opened his sack in the *inn*."

These were resting places for the night, the caravan houses, but they were not found at the end of every journey.

The inns were open to everyone from all parts of the country, all night, and never closed to the poor. No matter how dirty or ragged or forsaken a man was he was always welcome at an inn. It was much like a home to these weary travellers, they met people from far countries and they talked and smoked and parted in the morning.

The inns or khans vary much in size and material; sometimes they are made of mud bricks, sometimes of stone, but the form of the khans is always about the same. A square or oblong court with one or even two stories above it. One of the sides has a large gate, there is a gallery all around the court and often the court has a fountain in it and a well with troughs to water the animals.

The apartments for the animals are opposite the gates. These are divided into rooms, each having a small raised platform for the men to sleep on who are in charge of the animals during the night.

Mangers or troughs are built against the walls, from which the animals eat. No matter if a man had riches or was the very poorest, the rooms were assigned as the travellers arrived and no one was favored more than another.

We see a flight of stone steps from the court going up to the rooms for the travellers. They are unfurnished, and the sojourner pays a very modest sum. His own servant, if he has one, cooks his meals. There is absolutely no privacy, and I doubt if these people ever desire to be alone.

He makes his bed on the floor, with a mat or rug, covers his head with his cloak and goes to sleep. A fire is burning on a bare stone hearth and here the robber, the trader, the rich man, poor man, beggar, and the dervish dwell together absolutely indifferent to each other's circumstances.

There are no other kinds of inns known to the people there, these just suit their ways of living and their independence; they would not likely tolerate any other style. And to just such an inn or kahn, God sent His Son with "no place to lay His head."

"The Key Will I Lay Upon His Shoulder"
(Isaiah 22:22)

"The key of the house of David will I lay upon his shoulder."

It is quite the custom in the Orient for people to carry their key on their shoulder. The handle is made of brass or silver, or wood, and often very elaborately carved. The corner of the handkerchief is tied to the ring, and the key is then placed on the shoulder, and the handkerchief hangs down in front. Sometimes you will see men with a huge bunch of these large keys, then they will have half on one side of the shoulder and half on the other side. For a man to be marching along with a large key on his shoulder shows that he is certainly a person of importance.

"Whose key have you on your shoulder?" he would be asked. The key of the house of King David was to be on the shoulder of Eliakim.

There are still many buildings in Palestine which have enormous locks, with keys of course in proportion. Many of them are a real load to carry. The locks are made so that no false key could fit them, and they become more complicated in proportion to the number and position of the *wards* into which the metal drops are required to fall.

These huge locks are found on the inside of doors of gardens and outer courts, and inner rooms too. The only way the owner can unlock them is to cut a hole in the door, put his arm through the hole, and insert the key. Many of the garden doors are locked this way today.

In the Song of Solomon the bride says, "My beloved put his hand by the hole of the door," that he might enter.

The House Top
(Matt. 24:17)

The homes in the East with their flat roofs offer a place of quiet, such as you find nowhere else. There is often an upper room on the roof reached only by an outside staircase.

In a large well-to-do home these upper rooms would be the most spacious of the home, and the most suitable as guest chambers. At a great feast like the Passover many guests could be accommodated.

As the natives do not remove their clothing at night, they do not need much privacy, and a large number of strangers would see nothing unusual in occupying a room in common.

"They Uncovered the Roof"
(Mark 2:4)

"And when they could not come nigh to him for the press, they uncovered the roof where he was: and when they had broken it up, they let down the bed wherein the sick of the palsy lay."

Scripture tells that there was such a large crowd that the four men who carried the sick man could not force their way through, so they did just what a native would do, went up the outside stairs to the roof, broke up part of the roof, and lowered the sick man down in front of Christ. Oh, the homes are not like ours, but very low, with flat roofs. Jesus was probably standing in the open "lewan," a sort of vestibule in front of the house, with the roof over it, but no door. Those who carried the sick man, not being able to "come at him for the press," went to the roof and removed as much of that as was necessary and let the sick man down at Jesus' feet. It would be an easy matter to do in that kind of house; the roof is not high, and by stooping after they had removed a piece of the roof and holding the corners of the bed or couch — which was merely a thickly padded quilt, such as people still use in that region — letting the palsied man down would be rather a simple affair. The peasants are accustomed to opening their roofs to let down grain, straw and other articles. We have often seen it done.

The materials used for the roofs are beams about three feet or more apart, across which are arranged short sticks quite close together, and then covered with thickly matted thorn bush called *bellan*. Over this is spread a coat of mortar which is covered with earth and rolled flat and smooth. Any part of this could be removed without harming the rest, and no objection whatever would be made by the owners of the house. All men did was to scrape back a part of the earth over the lewan where Christ stood, remove the thorns and the short sticks and let down the man on the quilt at the feet of Jesus.

Afterwards they would repair the roof, restoring as before. Not all the roofs are made like this, but of material

Upper Left
"A heavy burden." A common sight in Palestine.

Upper Right
Carpenter at work. He uses his foot to hold the piece of wood he is working on. A daily sight in Nazareth.

Center Left
Woman preparing a meal in firepot with thorns. "The grass of the field."

Lower Left
"Men as trees walking." Men scarcely discernible under their loads, carrying brushwood and thorns.

more easily removed. The roof may have been made of coarse matting, or it may have been of boards or stone slabs, that could very easily have been lifted for the time being.

Anyway, the roofs are very low and flat, easily reached by stairs from the yard or court, and are very easily opened. You or I could with little difficulty open a roof as these four men did.

A Strong Tower
(Prov. 18:10)

"The name of the Lord is a strong tower: the righteous runneth into it, and is safe."

The law of retaliation in the East places upon the nearest relative the duty of killing the slayer. It matters not whether the death results from an accident or a planned murder. The Mosaic code provided six Cities of Refuge, three in convenient places on each side of the Jordan River, where the slayer could find shelter from the blood avenger. He would not be allowed to leave the City of Refuge during the life of the officiating high priest. After the high priest died, the penalty was remitted. These cities were not planned to shield the murderer, but to protect him until he had a trial, and if he was found guilty, he must pay the penalty.

However, that was not all the protection given. A man running for his life, could, if overtaken, call upon the name of some great sheikh, thus placing himself under the protection of this man, even if he did not know him personally.

If the avenger of blood, in spite of this appeal, slays the fleeing murderer, then honor demands that the sheikh who was called upon, have the avenger of blood put to death, or infamy would rest upon *his* name.

"The name of the Lord is a strong tower: the righteous runneth into it, and is safe."

"Thy Word Is a Lamp Unto My Feet"
(Psalm 119:105)

"Thy word is a lamp unto my feet, and a light unto my path."

Several years ago we were on our way from Emmaus to Jerusalem late at night, traveling on donkey back. As we rode along we noticed a path at a distance, but leading to ours, along which some men were walking. As they approached us, we noticed that as they walked over this narrow, stony path, filled with holes and many good places to stumble, a little light kept shooting out before them.

We waited until they joined us and found they had small foot lamps. Some had straps tied around the ankle with a small clay lamp attached; others were larger clay lamps carried in the hand. They would swing the lamp a few feet before them to throw a light on the stony, unsafe path. "Thy word is a lamp unto my feet, and a light unto my path." God does not promise light for a mile ahead or a half mile, but for one step at a time.

"Rachel Took the Images"
(Gen. 31:34)

"Now Rachel had taken the images, and put them in the camel's furniture, and sat upon them."

This appears to be the first notice we have of the existence and worship of these teraphim. Later on they were frequently mentioned, but here we see them first in this patriarchal family.

They were very small and easily hidden under the saddle bags of the camel. The Arabs still often hide stolen property under their saddles. Stealing a god to worship did not seem a bit strange to them. They would tell you that it was not a sin to steal a god who would help you get other things you wanted and needed.

Teraphim were frequently consulted for answers about the future by the children of Israel. After they entered the promised land, one of their corrupt practices was the worship or use of the teraphim. Many of the Hebrews leaned to idolatry then and consulted these images of gods, but still held on to their belief in the God of Israel.

Rachel stole the family gods or teraphim. We may wonder why such an ado was made over a pair of small figurines of very little money value. Well, we have learned from a clay tablet that an archaeologist found: "If a son-in-law possessed the household gods of his father-in-law, then he was considered a real son and shared in the inheritance." Rachel stole the family gods to make her husband an immediate member of her father's family, and that made him an heir and gave him a claim to a portion of Laban's property. Her husband had served the father-in-law fourteen years for the two daughters and she felt he had a right to be considered an heir.

Bed

We have only one reference to a bedstead in Scripture, that associated with the giant king Og (Deut. 3:11). It was evidently something very unusual in those days. The bed we read of in the Bible was two forms. One is the divan, used most in cities, and in the interior of a house; it would almost never be seen on a housetop where the people slept much of the year. The divan is a long, narrow mattress, usually stuffed with straw. In a poor home merely the sacking is seen; people better off would have the sacking covered with a bright gay material, or with a homemade rug. In the daytime these mattress divans are used as a lounge, usually on the floor around the side of the room, at night they would be placed over the floor, as the living room is generally the sleeping-room also. Psalm 149:5 sounds strange to a Western ear: "the saints . . . sing aloud upon their beds." It means simply that they were reclined on the divan or thin mattress or rug during the hours of rest in the hot part of the day, as they do even today.

When Esther received Haman at the feast (Esther 7:8), it was not really a bed that he fell upon, but the seat, the divan or rug which was used for a seat or for reclining during the day and was used as a bed at night. The bedchamber, like the one in which Joash was hid (II Kings 11:2), was a sort of cupboard place with usually an arched top, in which all the thin mattresses or rugs are piled up at night. This arrangement is very common in the East even now. The ordinary bed, used by most of the Orientals, the Bedouins, and the poorer classes in the cities and in every house, on the roof or in the court, is what we would call a mat. It was usually made from the dwarf-palm, or of tent cloth or grain bags or camel bags. This is unquestionably the bed of the New Testament. "Take up thy bed and walk"—a thing even a small child could easily do.

Bottles
(Mark 2:22)

The bottle of the Bible ever has been and is the skin of the boat, sheep, calf or kid. The Arab has an interesting way of removing the skin from the carcass of the animal. The head and the lower joints of the legs are removed; then the slow process of stripping the carcass of its skin begins. No tool or knife is used, it is all done by the hand and fingers. Once they have the covering of the upper part of a front leg clear, they use it as a tube and blow with all their strength through it, which loosens here and there, the hide from the flesh. Natives never remove a skin in any other way. The goat skin is the most in demand; it serves for water carrying, the four legs being tightly tied up. This skin is also used for oil, and in Bible times for wine (II Sam. 16:1; Jer. 13:12; I Sam. 1:24).

The Bedouins use these skins also as churns. In that case the hairy side is turned in, and serves as a friction for the production of the butter, which usually carries away with it a quantity of hair; however they always melt the butter down and strain it.

It is clear that our Lord referred to skin bottles in Matt. 9:17. After a skin had been expanded by wine, which would gradually ferment, it would then be used for water or oil (also see Job 32:19). After the skin of the sheep is removed from the carcass, the wool is cut off; these skins are as a rule used for grain and flour. The skin of the kid is used as a scrip. It is necessary to smoke, salt, and sun dry these skins before they are fit for use. (Psa. 119:83). When a skin is full it is of very great weight. The women prefer to carry a waterpot full on the head rather than a skin full on the back (Gen. 21:14). A calf's skin is used to carry liquids on the back of a camel.

Cruse of Oil
(I Kings 17:12; Matt. 25:4)

A small jar with a rounded bottom, at hand in every house in case of going out at night to a neighbor's house. The little lamp soon consumes what it contains, and it would be necessary to replenish it before returning home. The light of a lamp is not extinguished; it would be left burning during the visit if its oil permitted. The cruse contains a supply to replenish the lamp. The foolish virgins were unwise to go out without their cruse of oil.

CHAPTER 7

FEASTS

"Use Hospitality One to Another"
(Gen. 18:1-8)

"**B**E not forgetful to entertain strangers: for thereby some have entertained angels unawares" (Gen. 19:1-3; Judges 6:11-19; Heb. 13:2; I Peter 4:9).

We are reminded of Abraham, who entertained the three angels at his tent door; — of Lot, who prepared a feast for the two angels in Sodom; — and of Gideon, who made ready the kid and the unleavened cakes for the angel of the Lord at Ophrah. Such instances also give point to the Apostle's exhortation, "Use hospitality one to another, without grudging."

Dipping the Sop
(Matt. 26:23)

"He that dippeth his hand with me in the dish."

Orientals sit on the *deewan* around a small circular table or a tray made of heavy metal. The food is all placed in this tray or dish, and all dip into it in common. They break off a small piece of bread, fold it up to act as a spoon, and with this and their fingers they convey the food to the mouth. To eat with a person in the East implies a much closer bond of friendship than it ever does in our country. To break such a bond is almost unthinkable. The greatest mark of esteem a host can pay his guest is to select a choice morsel out of the common dish and place it in his guest's mouth.

The sop which our Lord gave to Judas was the greatest expression of love that He could show him, and no doubt, a last attempt to call Judas to a sense of the awful sin he was soon to commit.

Calling to a Feast
(Luke 14:17)

When a sheikh invites to a feast, he always sends a servant to call his guest at the proper time, "Come, for the supper is now ready."

This custom is confined to the wealthy. It is true now, as then, that to refuse the invitation is a high insult to the maker of the feast. The poor, the maimed, the halt and the blind, are on all the streets and what the man in the parable did, to call in these people when the first called refused, is just what would happen today, to show the extent of their benevolence, the depth of their humility. This parable in all its details is in close conformity to the customs of the East.

Table or *Scamba*
(John 13:23)

The Hebrews in the time of Christ had adopted the custom of reclining at the table on cushioned divans, resting themselves on the left arm. The tables were in three sections, forming three sides of a square, the seats being placed along the outer sides, — the servant waiting on the inside. Generally, though not invariably, each table held three persons only.

The seat of honor was that on the right side of the host, who sat in the center of the cross-table; the honored guest thus reclined, as it were, on the bosom of his host.

John 13:23, "Now there was leaning on Jesus' bosom one of his disciples, whom Jesus loved."

The general custom then and today is to bring a stool about fourteen inches high into the common sitting-room. On this is placed a tray of metal, usually copper, upon which the food is arranged. The bread is placed on a straw mat beneath the tray, and a cruse of water stands close by, from which all drink as they need. Around this stool and tray the guests gather, sitting on the floor while eating.

The dishes are generally stews of rice, cracked wheat (*burgul*) or beans, with plenty of sauce or soup with it. It is served in a deep dish or large bowl. They double up bits of thin bread, spoon fashion, and dip them into the dish. There is frequent reference to this custom in the Bible. They have neither knives nor forks, and they would not know how to use them. This is a very simple way to live; but they will tell you that is all they desire, and is much more convenient than our custom, and certainly less expensive.

High tables and chairs would be out of place and surely in the way. They do not have separate rooms in which to eat, hence they want a table that can easily be brought in and then removed.

They all eat out of the same dish and say to you, "Why not?" As their meat, when they have any, is always cooked up into stews, or else cooked until it is ready to fall to pieces, knives and forks are not needed; and when they have chicken or sheep, the flesh is easily torn to pieces with their fingers.

If you are a guest in their home, the polite Oriental will tear up the best bits and put them into your mouth. I have had this done for me by hands none too clean. Once my hostess placed some bits of meat in her own mouth and evidently found the taste extra fine, so she immediately removed the choice morsel and placed it in my mouth. . . . Well, you must look pleased and honored.

In their own way their cooking is good and their set-out respectable. The poorer people have no table, just a grass mat which they place on the earth floor, all sitting around the mat eating from the common dish.

"If His Son Asked Bread, Will He Give Him a Stone?"
(Matt. 7:9)

There are round flat stones in the wadies and brooks and other places which look so much like the Easterner's loaves of bread that no one could tell one from the other without touching them. That was likely why the Lord said, "If his son ask bread will he give him a stone?"

"Go Ye Into the City, and There Shall Meet You a Man With a Pitcher"
(Mark 14:13· Luke 22:10)

This does not seem like a very good description of the identity of the Lord's host, but when we remember that a man never, or at least rarely, carries water in a pitcher, then we understand more clearly. It is the women who carry all the water supply for the house. It is never a man's work, though he may carry a water-skin through the streets selling water, but never in an earthen vessel or pitcher for home use.

"So Shall He Sprinkle Many Nations"
(Isa. 52:15)

When a feast is given, a servant stands at the door with perfumed liquids such as rose water or orange blossom water, and sprinkles the guests as they enter. This sprinkling is understood to fit them for the presence of the entertainer, to declare them his guests, and, as such, to place them under his favor and protection.

I knew nothing of this custom and when entering a home to attend a wedding, was somewhat startled when a shower of rosewater went over my head, face and clothing. Then a friend explained that the perfuming fitted me for the marriage feast and made me a guest.

The prophet Isaiah no doubt had this in mind, when he said, "So shall he sprinkle many nations."

Arab Hospitality

"Peace Be Between Us."

Hospitality of the Arab tribes is remarkable. An Arab, on arriving at a strange camp, goes to the first tent that is convenient. He does not wait to be invited in, but without any ceremony, makes his camel lie down, unloads at the entrance, and entering the tent with the salutation of "Peace be between us," seats himself down by the fire, no matter whether the host be at home or not. Should the host be present, he will put fresh wood on the fire and begin to burn and grind coffee, offering his pipe to the guest. His wife, or wives, after spreading mats on the ground, if they have any mats, for the stranger to sit on, retire to the woman's part of the tent, which is divided in the center by sacks of corn, and whatever other effects they have. The women prepare the dinner or supper, without any order being given by the master, but as a matter of course. The coffee being ready, the host pours out for everyone. As soon as the meal is ready, he pours water alternately for his guests, who therewith wash the right hand; beginning with one, and going regularly round the circle. The ablution finished, everyone begins to eat. The host retires, not eating with his guests, but welcoming them with frequent repetition of "Coula, coula" (eat it all, eat it all).

The supper being finished, the master washes the hands of his party, and then eats what remains.

We know people who arrived at an Arab camp late at night when it was bitterly cold. The owner, his wife and children were all in bed. With the greatest of good humor everyone arose, kindled a fire. The wife kneaded the dough and prepared a supper. They all seemed to take everything as a matter of course and appeared to enjoy it. Such is Bedouin hospitality, and very different from that of the townsmen.

He who first sees a stranger from afar, and exclaims, "There comes my guest," has the right to entertain him, whatever tent he may alight at. We have had a lamb killed for us, which was an act of very great hospitality; for these people are poor.

Eaters of Barley Bread
(Judges 7:13, 14)

The common bread—such as was used by the very poor and unfortunate, or in times of famine—was made of barley. The Lord fed the hungry multitude with five barley loaves which belonged to a small boy. The sons of the prophets in the days of Elisha ate barley bread. Nothing was more common than for the people to complain that their oppressors had left them nothing but barley bread to eat. The Bedouins often called their enemies "eaters of barley bread."

The diet of the East has always been light and simple. The chief points of contrast between their diet and ours are the very small amount of animal food consumed and the variety of articles used with bread; but the chief point of agreement is the huge consumption of bread.

The preparations of bread were various and simple. Sometimes the fresh grains, after being carefully picked, were roasted in a pan over a fire, and eaten as "parched corn" in which form it was and is an ordinary article of diet.

I have watched women in Syria make bread a great many times. First they made a fire of dried dung and withered vine branches, which were laid upon the hearth; and the bread, being spread out with the hands like a pancake, was baked over this. Each cake was exceedingly thin, and could be rolled up and placed in the mouth at once.

Sometimes they made unleavened wafers, anointed with oil, which were baked in a plate or pan; and likely the cakes which Sarah made upon the hearth for the three angels, were of this kind (Gen. 18:6). Sometimes the grain was bruised and dried in the sun; then eaten, either mixed with oil, or made into soft cakes (the "dough" of the Old Testament).

The common people have little other food than durra bread, which consists of a sort of coarse millet, kneaded with camel's milk, oil, butter, or grease.

The best bread—such as was used in the sacred offering —was always made of wheat, and then ground and sifted formed the "fine flour" used in the offering. The ground but unsifted wheat would answer to the "flour" and "meal" of Judges 6:19.

In villages the bread is either baked on cakes of dried dung, or by means of clay ovens, built on the floor of the house. Each household possessed such an article except the very poor, when one oven sufficed for several families. It was heated with dried twigs and grass and thorns. The bread to be baked was placed both inside and out.

"And They Sighed for the Cucumbers"
(Num. 11:5)

The Israelies, when in the wilderness, "sighed for the cucumbers, and the melons, and the leeks, and the onions, and the garlic, which they had eaten in Egypt."

On the monuments in Egypt you find vegetables presented to the gods, especially leeks and onions, which were tied up in fancy shapes. Among the gifts of Rameses III to his gods, are "onions, 180 ropes, 50 sacks," with two other measures unknown. In Herodotus we read that the cost of radishes, onions, and garlic, for the workmen engaged upon one of the pyramids of Cheops, was 1600 silver talents.

Sometimes the food of the natives consists only of stewed vegetables, such as onions, lettuce, cucumbers, with parched corn. These onions are not like ours at all, but are exceedingly mild and delicious, said to be superior to any in the world. They are not covered with skins, but every part of them is soft and digestible. Lentils are also much eaten; melons, gourds, beans, pulse, lupines, cucumbers and dates as well.

"His Birthright for a Mess of Pottage"
(Gen. 25:29-34)

Pottage is another very common dish in the Bible Lands. The people call it *kool*. It is much like gruel and is made of various kinds of grain, which have been beaten in a mortar. The red pottage is made of *kurakan* and other grains, but it is not superior to the other. For such a mess Esau sold his birthright! When a man has sold his fields for an insignificant sum, the people say, the fellow sold his land for pottage." Does a father give his daughter in marriage to a low-caste? "He has given her for pottage." Has a learned man stooped from what was expected of him?— "He has fallen into the pottage-pot." Of a man in great poverty, they say, "Alas! he cannot get pottage." And Esau sold his birthright for a mess of pottage.

CHAPTER 8

FIELDS

"The Grass of the Field"
(Matt. 6:30)

"IF God so clothe the grass of the field, which today is, and tomorrow is cast into the oven . . ."

Before the rains come the whole mountain sides are covered with thorns which look like grass, and the natives call it so. The women gather these thorns for fuel. In many villages it is the only fuel they have. The women place it under their "fire pot" made of clay, and place on that the clay dish in which they cook their food.

"While Men Slept, the Enemy Sowed Tares"
(Matt. 13:25)

"Let both grow together until the harvest: and in the time of harvest I will say to the reapers, Gather ye together first the tares, and bind them in bundles to burn them: but gather the wheat into my barn."

The tare or *darnel* abounds all over the East, and is a great trial to the farmer. The grain is small and is arranged along the upper part of the stalk, which stands perfectly erect. The taste of the grain is bitter and if mixed with wheat in bread causes dizziness, and often acts as a violent emetic. It is a poison and must be carefully winnowed and picked out of the wheat or the flour is not fit for food. The tares can hardly be distinguished from the wheat until the heads appear at harvest time, — even the farmer cannot tell them apart. As harvest approaches the wheat grows heavy and bends over more and more, but the tares or darnel are so light-headed they stand very straight. At harvest time the farmer cuts the heads off the tares and puts them in a pile until he has harvested the wheat; then the tares are burned. "Let both grow together until the harvest: and in the time of harvest I will say to the reapers, Gather ye first the tares, and bind them in bundles to burn them: but gather the wheat into my barn."

Bread in Bible Lands
(John 6:35)

Our Lord's frequent references to Himself as the Bread of Life were full of meaning to the people to whom He spoke. Bread is sacred in Palestine, as the main article of food. An Arab would stop in the road to pick up a bit of bread that had fallen there, touch his forehead with it in token of respect, and carefully place it in a cleft of the wall or a rock, so that it would be safe from passing feet.

Native bread is usually a round, flat cake, from a quarter of an inch to an inch thick. Leavened bread is very little used among the peasants. The women cook the bread fresh for each meal. The oven is often a piece of sheet iron, slightly convex. It is upheld on three stones and a fire burns underneath. The woman puts a very thin, large piece of unleavened dough on the oven and after being cooked it looks much like a huge pancake. Sometimes they build a fire in a hole in the floor of their tent and fill the hole with small stones. The bread is placed on the hot pebbles. Sarah baked her bread on hot stones on the hearth in her tent.

Parched Pulse
(II Sam. 17:28)

The word pulse is found in Daniel 1:12, 16. It is very much cultivated in Palestine, and the whole plant being roasted, is sold in small bunches on the street as the peasants are very fond of it. It has a very large amount of concentrated nutriment, so that the Bedouin sometimes goes on a several days' journey with only a handful of pulse in his scrip for food. When King David fled from Absalom to Mahanaim, the people gave him as a present, "parched corn, beans, lentils, and parched pulse" (II Sam. 17:28).

Daniel 1:12 says, "Prove thy servants, I beseech thee, ten days; and let them give us pulse to eat, and water to drink."

Pulse looks something like very large peas.

Ruth Gleaning

(Ruth 2:5)

"Then said Boaz unto his servant that was set over the reapers, Whose damsel is this?"

This scene could easily be enacted at the present day by the people of Bethlehem. The salutations are the same between the owner and his servants, "The Lord be with you" is merely the *"Allah m'akum,"* heard every day, and the reply, "The Lord bless thee."

The reapers are apt to be rude to defenceless women, hence Boaz commanded them to be respectful to Ruth. The reapers come from all parts of the country, and largely from the lower class. Being far from home they throw off all restraint and do somewhat as they please.

The meals too, are the same today; the dipping the morsel in vinegar, and the parched corn — not like our corn or maize, but more like wheat or barley. A quantity is plucked with the stalks attached, they are tied into small parcels, a blazing fire is kindled with thorn bushes, and the corn heads are held in it until the chaff is burned off. The grain is then eaten and people all over the country are exceedingly fond of it.

Nor is the gathering of this corn for parching ever considered stealing. After roasting, the kernels are rubbed out

Upper Left

The potter at the wheel. Clay
in the potter's hands.

Upper Right

Vessel with the potter's plan
drawn — but not yet finished —
the flames have not yet done
their work.

Center Right

Vessel that has never been in
the furnace.

Lower Right

A Holy Vessel. This has been through the furnace
several times.

in the hand and eaten. Parched corn is often referred to in the Bible. You often see people as they pass along the wheat fields, pluck off some corn, rub the heads in their hands, and eat the grains unroasted, just as the apostles did. This also is allowable. The Pharisees had no objection to the disciples taking a few grains of corn; it was customary and allowed, but their objection was because it was done on the sabbath.

The owners often sleep on the summer threshing floors, just as the wealthy Boaz did when Ruth came to him. Though it is not allowable that a woman in general should sleep on these floors, and to do so would produce the same bad impression which Boaz feared, yet it is not unusual for husband, wife and children to encamp on the threshing-floor until the harvest is over. Doubtful characters come to the floors today, and did three thousand years ago in Bethlehem.

Because it was improper for single women to stay on the floors at night, why did Boaz say to Ruth, "All the city of my people doth know that thou art a virtuous woman?"

Boaz knew her character and that she was guided in her actions by her mother-in-law, who taught her that she had a right to Boaz for her husband, and that the law of God forbade her to marry any one else.

We again hear Boaz saying to Ruth, "When thou art athirst, go unto the vessels and drink, . . . At meal time . . . eat of the bread, and dip thy morsel in the vinegar . . . and he reached her parched corn, and she did eat."

This is a picture we saw in Palestine many times. Water is always present in large jars. The natives are fond of acids, and while usually they are satisfied with bread alone or a few olives or an onion, at harvest time they have a better meal. Tomatoes cut up with oil to dip and moisten their morsel in, or *leban,* a sour, clabbered milk, are favorites. Then they sit on the ground around a common bowl and dip in.

During barley harvest the wheat is still in the milk, and *"freaky"* (meaning rubbed wheat), is made extensively. This freaky is the parched corn of the Bible, in Hebrew *"gali."* The green wheat is cut and mixed with a pile of dry barley straw, which when set ablaze, is of sufficient quantity to roast the green wheat. They then rub these ears of wheat together in their hands and winnow out the dross.

The reapers still, as in the days of Boaz, make parched corn a part of their meal, for it is very delicious when eaten fresh.

It is still a very common sight to see wayfarers stopping along the road, cutting a handful of wheat from someone's patch, making a little parched corn for a meal, or just rubbing out the green ears in the hand to eat the soft kernels. (Deut. 23:25) : "When thou comest to the standing corn of thy neighbor, then thou mayest pluck the ears with thine hand, but thou mayest not move a sickle in thy neighbor's standing corn."

"Jesus went on the sabbath day through the corn; and his disciples were an hungered, and began to pluck the ears of corn, and to eat." This was a legitimate practice; the Pharisees were complaining only of the disciples breaking the sabbath (Matt. 12:12) .

"Thou Shalt Not Remove Thy Neighbor's Landmark"
(Deut 27:17)

There are certain parts of Palestine held in permanent ownership, but in the northern part of the country each farmer has his land assigned to him for one or two years, the amount being measured by a cord of a certain length, which is according to the number of members in his family, and his ability to cultivate it. This must be a very old custom, for the land was distributed in this manner among the

Hebrews in the days of Joshua, their inheritance being divided to them "by line."

In Psalm 78:55 we read, "He divided them an inheritance by line, and made the tribes of Israel to dwell in their tents."

Among the Assyrians, in the days of Judah, we find these fatal words, "Thou shalt have none that shall cast a cord by lot in the congregation of the Lord" (Micah 2:5).

When the time of the year for the "lot" is due, all the men who desire to take part meet on the threshing floor, where the chief man of the town or village awaits them with a bag of small stones. On each stone he has written the name of a field or portion of a field, the "lot."

Many of the fields now have names similar to those in use during the time of our Lord. There is the "Field of Blood," "Field of the Fight," "Field of the Rocks," and many others.

After all the men arrive, the Chief calls a small boy, far too young to know what it all means. The lad takes a pebble out of the bag and hands it to one of the men, and continues doing so until are supplied. Not one of the men can read, he does not understand where his lot is situated, but when he receives the stone from the child he says, "This is my lot, may God maintain it." A thought something like this is found in the sixteenth psalm, and the fifth verse, "Thou maintainest my lot."

The Chief then reads the name of the field which is written on each stone, so that every man knows the portion of land assigned to him for the coming year.

The lot may be a long way from his dwelling, so that it will take him hours to reach it each morning and make him very late arriving home at night. The lot may be exceedingly rocky, barren and unproductive, where, work as hard as he is able, there will be but little raised. The lot may be the very last thing and place he would desire, but he takes it quietly. If unlucky one year, he looks forward to something more favorable next year.

David is no doubt thinking of these people when he rejoices that his "lines are fallen unto me in pleasant places; yea, I have a goodly heritage" (Psalm 16:6).

In some places the land is divided in a very strange way. Facing the road would naturally be the most desirable for a lot, so the Chief would divide the lots so that only a very small breadth of the land would be allowed each man; one half line or perhaps up to two lines facing the road would run back almost indefinitely, so that a farm may be but a rod or two wide, and very, very long.

Then to make sure that each man knows the size of his land, the old landmarks are looked over and marked by a double furrow, one furrow twice the width of the others; and to make it doubly sure, they place at each end a heap of stones which they call the "stones of the boundary." Later on, if the furrow should disappear, the landmark of stones is still there.

We can understand how easily those boundary stones could be changed by a jealous and dishonest neighbor, even if it was forbidden by the law of Moses. It is still, as in the time of Moses, an unlawful and accursed act to remove the neighbor's landmark. There are no government surveyors or maps to which appeal can be made in case of disputed boundary lines. Furrows made by the plow for division are easily filled up, and the most common landmarks of mere piles of stones balanced one upon another, which a child could remove or knock down; yet they are respected and left untouched from generation to generation. "Thou shalt not remove thy neighbor's landmark, which they of old have set in thine inheritance" (Deut. 19:14; 27:17).

"They Shall Still Bring Forth Fruit in Old Age; They Shall Be Fat and Flourishing"
(Psalm 92:14)

The olive tree, mentioned forty times in the Old Testament, is one of the very first trees named in the Bible. An olive leaf was brought to Noah's ark (Gen. 8:11). The olive is the most common cultivated tree in Palestine, producing abundant fruit and oil. One tree often furnishes from ten to fifteen gallons of oil.

Olives and bread constitute a large part of the food of the peasants. Olive oil was and is today used very much for lighting. In the service of the tabernacle, besides being used for light, it was one of the ingredients of the "Holy anointing oil" (Exodus 25:6; 30:24).

Olive oil was used in treating wounds (Luke 10:34). It was used for the head (Psa. 23:5), as an act of courtesy (Luke 7:46), as well as to anoint priests, kings, and prophets for service (Lev. 8:12; I Sam. 16:13; I Kings 19:16). Many references in Leviticus show how much use was made of oil in connection with offerings.

The olive tree has small white flowers in May, which fall readily (Job 15:33.) The fruit is gathered by beating (Deut 24:20) or shaking the tree (Isa. 17:6). The olive tree grows slowly, very often lives to a very, very great age, and bears fruit till the last, even when the trunk is nothing but a shell.

"The righteous shall still bring forth fruit in old age."

Hyssop — Zufa
(Ps. 51:7)

"Purge me with hyssop, and I shall be clean; wash me (with *zufa*, as the original gives) and I shall be whiter than snow" (Ps. 51:7).

Hyssop is used as a spice and also for its medicinal oil. — But to the prophets it represented meekness and modesty. They contrasted the hyssop with the cedar of Lebanon, the symbol of exaltation and pride (II Kings 14:9).

Hyssop is a very effectual purge — internal cleansing; zufa is a potent bleach — external cleansing. "Purge me with hyssop, and I shall be clean; wash me with zufa and I shall be whiter than snow."

The Snare of the Fowler
(Psalm 91:3)

"For man also knoweth not his time: as the fishes that are taken in an evil net, and as birds that are caught in a snare; so are the sons of men snared in an evil time, when it falleth suddenly upon them" (Eccl. 9:12).

The fowler places the snare where it will not be seen, in a place much frequented by birds.

The snare is not large, but it is sure, and if the bird comes near it, he becomes a captive. It will be completely covered with leaves or anything to disguise it, so the birds will not know there is any danger near until too late.

God has promised not only to keep us from dangers we can see and know about, but from the unseen dangers. "Surely he shall deliver thee from the snare of the fowler."

Elisha Plowing With Twelve Yoke of Oxen
(I Kings 19:19)

"Elisha was plowing with twelve yoke of oxen before him, and he with the twelfth."

We are apt to think that he had a team of twelve yoke of oxen with which he was working, but the picture is of twelve separate plows following one after another as closely as possible. We have seen a dozen of them at work like this.

Now the arable land of nearly all villages is cultivated in common. The Arab farmers delight to work together in companies, partly for protection, but more for their great love of gossip.

Their small plows make no real furrow, but merely scratch the soil, so any number may follow after, each making his own scratch, and they go back and forth until the whole piece of land is plowed. It was well that Elisha was last, for they may not pass one another. We can believe that Elisha's oxen and plow were like the ones in Palestine today. The people worked in companies then as they do now, and for the same reasons.

Weights and Scales
(Deut. 25:13)

"Thou shalt not have in thy bag divers weights (margin, stones) a great and a small."

In most countries money was originally paid out by *weight*. The standard unit of weight among the Jews was the shekel, which was represented in patriarchal days and for long after by a stone or stones of specific gravity. We read in Lev. 19:36, margin, "Just balances, just *stones,* a just ephah, and a just hin, shall ye have." (Deut. 25:13, margin; Prov. 20:10, margin).

As no two such weights were of similar appearance, and not all equally ponderous, even when of the same apparent size, the eye of the customer had no standard of estimate by which he might detect the trader's dishonesty, who used different weights for different occasions and customers. Hence the significance of the command in Deut. 25:13, "Thou shalt not have in thy bag divers weights (marg. stones a great and a small.")

The practice of weighing money is very ancient. In the account of the transaction between Ephron and Abraham, we read that the latter weighed to the Hittite landowner, as purchase money for the cave of Machpelah, "four hundred shekels of silver, current money with the merchants." (Gen. 23:16) ; and there is evidence to show that the practice continued till the time of Jeremiah.

The shekel was the standard weight of the Jews, so let us see how it stood in relation to their other weights. It "was divided into two *bekahs,* and the bekeh into ten *gerahs.* The talent equalled 3,000 shekels; and between the shekel and the talent came the "pound" or *maneh,* which according to Ezekiel 45:12 contained sixty shekels, though at other times it contained only fifty; and at one time no less than one hundred shekels.

During the winter of 1937-38, while living in the American Colony in Jerusalem, we were very much interested in the manner of measuring the value of wood which was brought there for sale. It was hard wood, mostly chunks and roots of the olive tree, fairly dry. There was in the back yard of the Colony an old crude pair of balances. The Arab who brought the wood on the back of his camel would place in one "pan" of the balances a rough rock which had been brought in from the field. Then he would fill the other pan until the balances balanced; then unload and repeat. As the weight of the rock represented a certain value in wood, and the arrangement had been agreed upon, all concerned seemed to be satisfied.

"He Drinketh Up Scorning Like Water"
(Job 34:7)

This idom is very common among the Arabs. It is natural to their mind to think of many operations under the idea of *eating* and *drinking,* which we connect with some other sense than that of taste. They very commonly speak of *eating* a great rain when they have been drenched in a shower; or they say they ate a strong wind or a very piercing cold. There are many, many other things that they will tell you they *drank* or ate.

"He drinketh up scorning like water."

A Bag With Holes
(Haggai 1:6)

"He that earneth wages, earneth wages to put into a bag with holes." God had commanded the children of Israel to repair the Temple and they disobeyed Him. They could earn more money in other kinds of work, and they probably said to each other, "There is no hurry about repairing the temple, it can wait for a while without doing any harm; our families need more and more; we have a good chance to earn big wages just now and it is surely our duty to look after our families first, to do our best for them.

Listen to what God thinks and says, "He that earneth wages, earneth wages to put into a bag with holes."

We see this same situation everywhere today. Church work neglected, people earning money on the Sabbath and their pew is empty. Does it ever occur to them that all that extra money may fall through holes? Unless we pay our debt to God first, we are apt to remain in debt to others. It always pays to obey God, to repair the temple, to put first things first.

CHAPTER 9

TOMBS AND TENTS

"She Covered Him With a Mantle"
(Judges 4:18)

" AND Jael went out to meet Sisera, and said unto him.
Turn in, my lord, turn in to me; fear not. And when
he had turned in unto her into the tent, she covered him
with a mantle."

This is very, very difficult for a Western mind to understand. In imagination let us make a visit to the camp of
some Bedouins and learn of their strange manners and
customs and something of their strange way of thinking and
doing things. To these people nothing would be more
natural than Jael's action. We must remember two things.
First, there is an unwritten law, yet one that even the most
unprincipled would never dare violate, the duty of enter-
taining strangers. You could not possibly pass an encampment of Bedouins without their coming out and inviting
you in to rest and using almost the same words, to you as
used by Jael, "Come in, my lord, come in and rest."

Secondly, no strange man is ever permitted to enter the
woman's part of the tent. They have another unwritten
law that such an offender is worthy of death, and any relative of the woman is obliged to carry this law into execution.

If a woman allowed a stranger to enter the woman's part
of the tent, she, too, would be worthy of death.

In Judges, fourth chapter, we are told that Sisera was escaping when he passed Jael's tent. She, with true hospitality, invited him to come in and rest. She, of course, expected him to enter the men's or public part of the tent only, as any man would do. Sisera wanted a good hiding place, and of course, no place could be safer than the woman's part of the tent for no Israelite would intrude there. Jael was not a Jewess, but a Kenite.

He, no doubt, pushed his way into the woman's section of the tent against Jael's wishes, for entering here was the greatest insult and exposed her to dishonor and also death. She is placed in an exceedingly hard position. If she ordered him to leave, he would likely have killed her to save his own life, while to allow him to stay, would have exposed her to the anger of her husband, who would at once condemn her as unfaithful, and stone her to death as the common law provided.

She decided she must protect herself, and when he fell asleep, she pinned him to the ground with the tent pins. She knew well how to use tent pins, for the women take down and put up the tents.

We are told that she gave him milk to drink when he asked for water. Water is scarce in that dry country and they would have goat's milk to drink, probably sour milk, *leben,* which is very refreshing.

Jael is called blessed in Judges 5:24, not because she committed murder, but because while defending her own character and her life too, she was ridding the Israelites of a very cruel tyrant.

Judges 4:3 says, "he mightily oppressed the children of Israel." The atrocities at which these words plainly hint are all known to Jael. Again and again she has been appalled by the tale. And here is the one man from whose planning brain and fearful will the whole have sprung. He is on the way to Hazor, Jabin's capital, where fresh forces await him. After rest he will go on and renew the conflict.

We do not need to be Israelites to feel the gratitude that glows in the word, "Blessed above women shall Jael the wife of Heber the Kenite be, blessed shall she be above women in the tent" (Judges 5:24).

The Needle's Eye
(Matt. 19:24)

"It is easier for a camel to go through the eye of a needle, than for a rich man to enter into the kingdom of God."

Let us examine a city gate which has the "needle's eye." City walls have several large gates of iron, which are always two-leaved. In Isaiah 45:1 we find these words: "I will open before him the two-leaved gates." When we read of Samson taking the "doors of the gate" it means he unhitched both leaves. (Judges 16:3) "And Samson arose at midnight, and took the doors of the gate of the city, and the two posts, and went away with them." Gates are closed at sunset and not opened until sunrise. This is still the case in all eastern walled cities.

When once the gates were shut, they would not be opened except to admit a great official who might be on an errand of importance. The chief captain sends Paul from Caesarea "at the third hour of the night" (Acts 23:23) —about 9 p. m. A wise precaution because no one could possibly pursue them until the gates were opened at about six the next morning. The apostle therefore had nine hours' start, which made it impossible for any one to overtake him on the way.

When any person has to be admitted or allowed to leave the city by night, a small door fixed into the larger one is opened. This smaller door was called the "needle's eye." Matthew 19:24 says, "It is easier for a camel to go through the eye of a needle." Now let us try to picture the scene to which Jesus refers. Camels laden with large bags of barley, wheat, charcoal, or wood, were coming into town daily.

The burdens are well balanced on either side of the camel's back, and stand out sometimes three or four feet on the right side and on the left. You can see, therefore, that a camel needs a wide gate to admit him and his great burden. Every traveler in the East knows from experience what it means to meet a camel coming along a street which is only just wide enough for the beast to pass through. You cannot stand against the wall; your only possible way to do is to stoop very low and allow the camel to pass by, the burden then being above you. Hence the meaning of the Lord's words was easily understood by His hearers. A camel with its burden cannot enter the needle's eye.

Jaffa Gate in Jerusalem has a very fine "needle's eye."

Maniacs in the Tomb
(Mark 5:2-16; Luke 8:26-36)

These are very sad but remarkable accounts of demon possession, and we are apt to pity, but to think that cases like these existed only in Bible days and Bible Lands; but there are very many similar today — furious and dangerous maniacs, who wander about the mountains and sleep in caves and tombs. At their worst they are unmanageable and have strength no normal person could ever possess.

I have seen cases that chains would not hold, they would snap a strong chain as we would a piece of string. Mark says they went naked — and they do today. It is one of the most common traits of demon possession that the victims refuse to wear clothes. A few months ago we visited a little mud-hut town where there were several demoniacs running naked, never speaking a normal language, but making noises like wild animals. They would eat only what they could steal, and their manner of eating was worse than that of a wild creature.

These poor wretches are held in very great reverence by Moslems, who, through some terrible perversion of ideas, believe them to be inspired and peculiarly holy. The manifestations of satanic power are so inhuman and terrible that no one seeing these poor creatures as we did could believe anything else but they were controlled by satanic spirits, and Mark and Luke knew what they were writing about.

No one is in a position to judge unless they have spent days or weeks among them. But — the Bible Lands with their caves and tombs do not have all the poor possessed maniacs.

Christ Three Days and Three Nights in the Heart of the Earth?

(Matt. 12:40)

This Scripture says Christ was, and according to the traditions of our church, our Lord was crucified on a Friday afternoon and then was raised from the dead very early Sunday morning. However, this is not three days and three nights. We notice that the Bible does not say He was crucified on Friday, but it does say He was crucified on "the day before the sabbath" (Mark 15:42). The Jewish sabbath began Friday night at sunset and lasted until Saturday at sunset, so we have naturally thought that Christ was crucified Friday. But, besides the weekly sabbath which fell on Saturday, the Jews had other sabbaths. The first day of their Passover week, regardless of what day it came, was always a sabbath (Exod. 12:16; Lev. 23:7; Num. 28:16-18).

Now we need to know whether the sabbath after Christ's Crucifixion was the weekly sabbath or was it the Passover sabbath? God's word does not leave us to guess about this important event, for John 19:14 tells us that the day of the trial and crucifixion was "the preparation of the Passover (R.V.). So we see it was not the weekly sabbath (Friday), but it was the day before the Passover sabbath, which fell that year on Thursday. This would prove beyond doubt that Jesus was crucified on Wednesday.

Astronomers have gone into this matter very thoroughly and have figured out in the year of the crucifixion, generally accepted as having been 30 A.D., that the moon was full on April 6, which was Thursday, and the day on which the Passover would have been celebrated. This would prove that our Lord Jesus was crucified on Wednesday.

Superscriptions on the Cross

(Matt. 27:37; Mark 15:26; Luke 23:38; John 19:19)

In Matthew 27:37 we read, "And set up over his head his accusation written, This is Jesus, the King of the Jews."

In Mark 15:26 we find, "And the superscription of his accusation was written over, The King of the Jews."

Luke 23:38 tells us, "And there was also a superscription written over him . . . This is Jesus, the King of the Jews." (R.V.)

Now we turn to John 19:19: "And Pilate wrote a title, and put it on the cross. And the writing was, Jesus of Nazareth, the King of the Jews."

No two of these agree. What is the difficulty? Can all four be correct? The answer is so very clearly given in these very passages. John 19:20, (R.V.), tells us that in order that all the people of different tongues might read it, the charge upon the cross on which Christ was crucified was written in Hebrew, in Greek, and in Latin; in Hebrew for the common people, in Latin for the Romans, and in Greek, as that was the universal language.

Matthew wrote especially for the Jews and gave the inscription as it was in Hebrew. Mark gave the inscription as it was in Latin, and Luke as it was in Greek. John gives it in the full Roman form, "Jesus of Nazareth." There is no difficulty at all if we notice exactly what the Bible tells us.

Impure Bible Stories

Unbelievers of different degrees are always saying that parts of the Bible are unchaste, and not fit to be read in a mixed audience. Well, there are chapters and verses that were not intended to be read in public, but these chapters are absolutely not filthy. To be sure, they speak in the very plainest terms of the vilest sins known, but only in order to expose their loathsomeness, and as a warning; but this is not impurity.

The way a story is told and for what purpose, makes it clean or vile. If the writer is making a joke of sin, it is then indecent. Sin is pictured and called by its right name in the Bible, and the terrible results related to make man with his sinful heart turn away from these sins.

The Bible was not all written for public reading, but it was written for a purpose. We have in our library several very valuable medical books, but there are pages and passages in them we would not think of reading in public; they were never written for that, but are excellent and very helpful in their own place and time. They are written to describe conditions that do exist, and they give warnings of what will come to pass if the warnings go unheeded. We wouldn't think of refusing to read and understand these valuable warnings just because we could not read them in public.

The Bible, too, has many warnings of what will happen if sin in the human heart is allowed to run its course, but that does not make the Bible an unclean book.

Only people with filthy minds can ever call the Bible filthy. Let us be as fair with God's Word as we are with other books that are written to help and warn humanity of the many dangers around us.

David's Sin

(II Sam. 11)

This chapter gives us the account of the downfall of a "man after God's own heart." He had been surrendered to the will of God, was a generous, kind man, and desired much to keep in God's plan for his life. But, he fell in a moment of weakness. He got his eyes off God and God's Word, he played with temptation; and one sin led to another to cover up the first. His sin led him down, down to the deepest depths of vileness and dishonor. He committed one of the most outrageous crimes one man ever committed against another.

There is no use trying to excuse this sin to sceptics, there is absolutely no excuse. God did not excuse him, but sent His prophet to rebuke him saying: "By this deed thou hast given great occasion to the enemies of the Lord to blaspheme" (II Sam. 12:14).

The people considered David a very great man, a great hero, and unless the Bible writers had been guided by God Himself, they surely would have tried to cover up David's contemptible sin. But the Bible does not do so, and thank God for it, the Bible exposes the sin and holds up the sinner as a warning.

David was forgiven, but he drank very deeply from the bitter cup he had prepared for himself. David suffered through his children what was just the fruit of his own terrible sin, and he was perfectly conscious of it.

This part of David's life story, however, has given hope to many a lost sinner to ask, "Is there pardon for me?" Yes, for you. David found mercy and pardon. So can any one who so desires.

CHAPTER 10

GATES AND TRADES

In the Gate of Samaria
(II Kings 7:1)

THE ancient custom of holding markets at gates still obtains in the East, and the people gather every morning to buy horses, mules, asses and camels. At sunrise the owners of the animals assembled and exhibited them for sale. But there were sellers of other goods, with stalls for their display.

The Seat of Justice
(I Sam. 4:18)

The gates being used as the place of judgment, a seat in the gate became a seat of honor and authority. The aged Eli (who had "judged Israel forty years") was sitting in the gate when the messenger arrived with the news that the ark of God was taken by the Philistines; and we are told that both Mordecai and Daniel sat in the king's gate, an expression which denotes the authority that was vested in them.

We learn also from Scripture that the husband of a virtuous woman was "known in the gates," when he sat "among the elders of the land" (Prov. 31:23). It is related of the Persians, that when one of their great men build a palace it is the custom to feast the king and his grandees in it for several days. "Then the great gate of it is open: but when these festivities are over they shut it up, never more to be opened." The custom is one of great

110

antiquity, and may, perhaps, be alluded to in the passage, "This gate shall be shut, it shall not be opened, and no man shall enter in by it; because the Lord, the God of Israel, hath entered in by it, therefore it shall be shut. It is for the prince" (Ezek. 44:2, 3).

"An Artificer in Brass and Iron"
(Gen. 4:22)

Tubal-cain, an instructor of every artificer in brass and iron," or "a whetter of every instrument of copper and iron." His brother, Jubal, was "the father of all such as handle the harp and organ." Tools were required for the construction of these instruments, and therefore the smith's art must have taken precedence.

The preparation of iron for use in war, agriculture or domestic purposes, was one of the earliest applications of labor, and, along with this was the use of copper alloyed with tin, that is, bronze, the "brass" of the Bible. The construction of so huge a vessel as Noah's ark shows us clearly that the smith's art made great progress at a very early age; but whether the metal used then was bronze or iron, we do not know. In the construction of the tabernacle no iron was found, though bronze is frequently mentioned.

After the children of Israel took possession of the land, the occupation of a smith became a very important trade. In the days of Saul it is mentioned that "there was no smith found throughout all the land of Israel (I Sam. 13:19), the reason being that the Philistines had either destroyed or removed all who followed that craft, likely to prevent them from possessing themselves of swords and spears. Nebuchadnezzar did the same. We read that he "carried away . . . all the craftsmen and smiths; and left only the poorest sort of the people of the land" (II Kings 24:14; Jer. 24:1).

The Jewish artificers were not, as the Romans and Greeks, servants and slaves, but men of some rank and wealth: In the New Testament we find that St. Paul, though of noble birth, was brought up to the craft of tent-making; and even now, almost every Jew, no matter what his prospects are, is instructed in some trade or profession.

The art of overlaying with gold was also known to the ancient Egyptians, as was proved some time ago by the discovery at Thebes of a mummy, which was entirely wrapped in plates of gold.

"And They Fetched the Carved Image"
(Judges 18:18)

Carving was one of the crafts of those days. In the Bible carving included all ornamental cutting of ivory, wood, or other hard material.

The carved relics of other days have been found in abundance in the ruins of ancient Nineveh and many other mounds. In one chamber in Nineveh were found two sitting figures, holding a scepter. The chairs on which the figures were seated and the robes on the figures were enamelled with blue let into ivory, and beside them were many figures all covered with gold leaf. They were elegant in design, and showed an intimate knowledge of the art of working in ivory.

There were winged sphinxes, lions, people, bulls, flowers, and all a most wonderful work of art.

Herodotus tells that in the temple of Belus at Babylon there were tables, thrones, couches of solid gold beautifully carved. Couches of ivory and silver, beds inlaid with gold, silver and ivory, have been found in those old tombs.

We think of the ivory throne of King Solomon, overlaid with gold, with its six steps and fourteen lions (I Kings 10:18-20).

"And Hiram Sent Masons"
(II Sam. 5:11)

We learn that the masons employed on King David's house were sent by Hiram. The monuments of Egypt, Nineveh, Ruins of Baalbek, and many other wonderful ruins of temples and palaces all bear witness to the wonderful skill of the masons of antiquity.

"The Carpenter Encouraged the Goldsmith"
(Isaiah 41:7)

Another of the handicrafts in Scripture is carpentry. The building of the ark is a proof of the progress of this art before the Flood; and on very ancient monuments we see pictures of hatchets, saws, chisels, oil-horns, planes, drills, mallets, rules, plummets, squares, and baskets of nails, used by the very ancient Egyptians.

We know that "the cabinet-makers of Egypt were not one bit behind the very best of these days, either in design or manual execution." They made boxes inlaid with different woods and some of ebony inlaid with ivory. Veneering and dovetailing were also known then. And we read, Isaiah 41:7, "They helped every one his neighbor. So the carpenter encouraged the goldsmith, and he that smoothed with the hammer, him that smote the anvil, saying, It is ready for the soldering; and he fastened it with nails, that it should not be moved."

Then in the New Testament there is Joseph the carpenter, the husband of Mary.

"Took Bread and a Bottle of Water"
(Gen. 21:14)

"And Abraham took bread and a bottle of water, and gave it to Hagar."

The bottles of the East are made of goatskins. When the goat is killed, the head and feet are cut off; then the carcass is drawn out of the skin by turning the skin inside out. It is then tanned, then the places where the head and tail were cut off are sewn together. It is then ready to be filled with water or wine. When filled, it is tied about the neck. The large bottles are he-goat skins and the smaller ones are kids' skins.

Doubtless this was the kind of bottle that Abraham gave to Hagar when he sent her away. Also this Scripture refers to a skin bottle: "No man putteth new wine into old bottles: else the new wine burst the bottles, and the wine is spilled."

After a time, the continual fires and smoke in an Arab tent dry and blacken his goatskin bottles. This illustrates the Psalmist's cry, "I am become like a bottle in the smoke" (Psa. 119:83). David had been living in Saul's palace where they used vessels of gold and silver. At this time he was compelled to live as the wild Arabs, and to drink, like them, out of a smoked goatskin bottle.

"Go Down to the Potter's House"
(Jer. 18:3, 4)

"Then I went down to the potter's house, and, behold, he wrought a work on the wheels."

Let us look into an Oriental pottery. You will see no machinery or fine buildings, just a plain shed. You see a wheel, and beside it a pile of clay and a dish of water. The potter takes a lump of clay in his hand, places it upon the wheel, which is revolving, and smooths it into a low cone; then, thrusting his thumb into the top of the cone, he opens a hole down through the center, and this he continually widens by pressing the edges of the revolving cone between his hands. As it enlarges, he gives it whatever shape he pleases with the utmost care and speed.

When Jeremiah was watching the potter, the vessel was marred in his hand, and so, "he made it again into another vessel, as seemed good to the potter to make it." We saw this happen many times. Because of some defect in the clay, the potter changed his mind, crushed the jar into a shapeless mass of clay, and beginning anew, fashioned it into a totally different vessel.

One is amazed at the quick performance, and at the result, until one remembers that the clay is in the hands of a master workman.

Now let us go into a peasant's home. As you enter, back of the door you will find a bench about four feet high, with three holes in it. This is the water-jar stand. It is called "the holder of jars." Here you will see two large jars, each holding four or five gallons, and beside them a small drinking vessel.

The peasant will offer you the small drinking vessel as you enter the house. It is very much of an art to be able to use it, but to people brought up from childhood in an Oriental home it does not appear so. You will be invited to fill it to the brim from the first jar, called the vessel of honor.

What is the vessel of honor? Well, let us go back to the pottery and ask to buy a vessel. The potter will ask, "Do you want to carry it to the fountain? Then you must bear a vessel of honor" (II Tim. 2:20, 21).

A vessel of honor, what does it mean? It is a vessel that will give out pure water to quench the thirst of the stranger and the weary traveler. You purchase the vessel of honor, holding about five gallons. It has two handles and is beautifully shaped. You place it on your right shoulder or your head and go to the fountain to get water.

If you meet a stranger he will see your jar filled with cold, clean, refreshing water, and he likely will ask for a drink. This is the mission of a "vessel of honor," giving free water, the gift of God, to passers-by. It is nothing but an earthen vessel, but nevertheless, it is a vessel of honor, because of its giving-out nature. It fulfills the expectation of the master potter.

This is the first large vessel on that bench behind the door. Next to that is another vessel. It looks just like the vessel of honor; but is not of the same nature. You could never tell the difference, but the potter can explain to you the difference between the vessel of honor and the vessel of dishonor.

This vessel will remain at home. All the stale water in the vessel of honor will be emptied into it. It receives *much,* but gives out very little.

In Jeremiah 22:28 we read of a vessel called "empty of pleasure." This is the vessel beside the vessel of honor on the bench. This vessel receives the left-over water, is forever receiving, but never gives out refreshing water. It is used for stale water only, and after a time the inside becomes slimy, and the water ill-smelling, and there is now no pleasure in it, either to the potter or to the owner. It is finally placed in the backyard as a receptacle for waste things and then will be called an abominable vessel. This is mentioned in Isaiah 65:4.

It must be sad for the potter to know that the vessel he spent much time and skill upon should become a vessel empty of pleasure, and at last become an abominable vessel.

Vessel of Mercy
(Rom. 9:23)

"And that he might make known the riches of his glory on the vessels of mercy, which he had afore prepared unto glory."

Here is a vessel of mercy.

A Moslem never prays without washing his hands. In the villages travelers need water supplied to them, so the villagers provide small vessels of water for the traveler to use called vessels of mercy, to help others.

Vessel of Wrath

(Rom. 9:22)

Let us return to the pottery. We see a pile of vessels laid aside, called vessels of wrath, useless to the potter. They appeared absolutely all right until they were put into the furnace. They came out cracked, they just could not stand the fire. However, the potter will not give them up, he has prepared a certain kind of cement out of blood from a small insect called the *fasuka* which lives on the body of a bull. The potter takes the blood of the fasuka and mixes it with some powdered broken pottery and cements the cracks in his vessel of wrath. When it passes through the furnace again, it may come out all right, or it may come out broken again. He patiently cements it again and again, but he may finally be obliged to lay it aside and pronounce it a vessel of wrath, of no value, and then he casts it away. Romans 9:22, "What if God, willing to show his wrath, and to make his power known, endured with much long suffering the vessels of wrath fitted to destruction."

A Clean Vessel

(Isa. 66:20)

"An offering in a clean vessel into the house of the Lord."

It was once a vessel of honor on that bench, giving out life-giving water to thirsty travelers. It has been handled by many unclean hands. Its nature is not changed, but its looks have been marred. So it will be taken to the potter again to be filed and scraped. He will remove all uncleanness left by contact with soiled hands, then place it in the furnace again, burn it once more.

It comes out for use again, clean without and within, "A Clean Vessel."

A Chosen Vessel
(Eph. 1:4)

Let us once more return to the pottery. Tell the potter that you are returning to your own country and desire to take home a vessel to show your friends. You request him to choose for you. He will hand you his chosen vessel, saying, "I will never be ashamed to send this vessel to any part of the world, for I have chosen it and I know it will never put me to shame. It is a chosen vessel.

"It may look the same to you as the other vessels; it may not seem very attractive, but it will stand the test.—It is a chosen vessel."

Holy Vessel
(Isa. 52:11)

"The vessel of the Lord."

It is a very sacred vessel. No one can handle it but those who are clean and fit to enter the house of the Lord.

"Clay in the potter's hand," to be made into vessels of honor, dishonor, wrath, mercy; broken, clean, chosen, holy — which? The choice remains in our power.

END